Irving Howe is Distinguished Professor of English at the City University of New York. Born in New York City in 1920, he is the author of many books including *Politics and the Novel*, *Steady Work*, *Decline of the New*, *Thomas Hardy*, *William Faulkner* and, most recently, *World of our Fathers*. He has co-edited several anthologies of Yiddish writing and is the editor of *Dissent* magazine.

TROTSKY

Irving Howe

Distinguished Professor of English,
City University of New York

THE HARVESTER PRESS
By agreement with Fontana

THE HARVESTER PRESS LIMITED
Publisher: John Spiers
2 Stanford Terrace, Hassocks, Sussex

Trotsky
This edition first published in 1978 by
The Harvester Press Limited
in association with Fontana Books.
Published simultaneously in paperback in
Great Britain by Fontana Books in their
'Modern Masters' series, edited by
Frank Kermode.

© Irving Howe 1978

British Library Cataloguing in Publication Data
Howe, Irving
  Trotsky.
  1. Trotsky, Leon
  320.5'32'0924   HX312.T75

  ISBN 0–85527–831–5

Printed and bound in Great Britain by
REDWOOD BURN LIMITED
Trowbridge and Esher

Contents

Preface

This is a small book on a large subject. I have written it for two reasons: first, as an introduction to the life and thought of a major twentieth-century figure, and second, as a political-intellectual criticism of his role in modern history and his commentaries upon it.

In a book of this size everything must be compressed. Much has been omitted which in a full-length biography or political study could not have been: e.g., discussion of Trotsky's writings on China, his numerous articles concerning revolutionary strategy in Europe during the twenties, his military writings, and his efforts to rebuild a revolutionary movement in the 1930s. But I make no pretence at being comprehensive. I have tried to stay with the main lines of Trotsky's intellectual development, those that may seem central to a serious reader of our moment.

Trotsky's ideas are inseparable from his career as Marxist revolutionary; they cannot, or should not, be considered in isolation, as a mere system; they take on vibrancy only when set into their context of striving, debate, combat. I have therefore provided a spare biographical frame, just enough narrative about his life to help bring out his ideas. But this is not a biography; it is a political essay with a narrative foundation.

There is, in any case, a major biography available, Isaac Deutscher's three volumes. I have borrowed from it liberally in telling the story of Trotsky's life, since I admire Deutscher's historical achievement quite as much as I disagree with some of his political opinions. Let me here express my gratitude to him for his masterful work.

It may help the reader to know that this book emerges out of a rather complicated intellectual relationship with its subject. Like other American socialists, I came for a brief time under Trotsky's political influence. Almost four decades have passed since that youthful experience, and since then, even though or perhaps because I have remained a socialist, I have found myself moving farther and farther away from his ideas. Yet he remains a figure of heroic magnitude and I have tried to see him with as much objectivity as I could summon.

In writing this book I have drawn upon an essay I wrote about Trotsky in the early 1960s, using some of its materials but revising a number of opinions. Since this book is about five times the length of the essay and a good many years have intervened between the two, it is only natural that there should be significant differences.

A word of thanks to several friends – Michael Harrington, Emanuel Geltman, Stanley Plastrik, Stephen Cohen, Michael Walzer – who have read all or parts of the manuscript. Many of their suggestions have helped me, but I alone remain responsible for errors of fact and mistakes of judgement.

1 Early Years, Basic Theories

For a young man of independent spirit growing up in late nineteenth-century Russia, rebellion was almost inevitable. Tsarist society lay besotted in backwardness. A glaze of obscurantism covered religious and moral life. Relations among people, especially in the countryside, were often openly brutal – brutal, so to say, on principle. The reigning autocracy believed it was right that the peasants be held down by whip and cross. If liberal, secular and rationalist ideas had begun to penetrate the thought of the intelligentsia, official Russia still looked with hatred on the Enlightenment and its values. Yet recent scholars are right in stressing that this was not a totalitarian society : it was neither efficient nor passionate enough for that, nor had it reached the point of sophisticated malevolence required for ideological and physical terror. In Tsarist Russia power showed itself as a naked fist, intent upon making itself an eternal presence : is if Asia were forever the fate of mankind.

Nevertheless, in the several decades before the First World War, Russian society was starting to experience major changes. Industries sprang up in the cities; workers learned to articulate their demands; revolutionary ideas slipped across the borders and into the minds of a fervent vanguard; parties were organized and allowed, more or less, to function. Perhaps the most significant energy of moral transformation came from the great Russian writers, whose work stimulated feelings of shame, conscience and idealism. In the tradition of moral seriousness that has characterized the Russian mind at its best, there grew up a community of readers and writers, together worrying, talking, thinking about the fate of their tormented nation.

It was into this Russia that Leon Trotsky was born. Lev Davidovich Bronstein (1879–1940) – only as a young revolutionist would he adopt the name of Trotsky – came from a family of well-to-do Jewish farmers living near the Black Sea. Among Russian Jews this was an unusual circumstance. To work a large farm rather than trading in a cramped ghetto town, to live as prosperous landowners who could mistreat peasants almost as freely as gentiles did, to abandon the religious pieties that still held many East European Jews in their grip – this way of life among the Bronsteins enabled their son all the more quickly to abandon the whole tradition of 'Jewishness' which the *shtetl* imposed even on its most 'liberated' children.

There appears to be some evidence that the young Bronstein picked up a few smatterings of Jewish education. After all, his parents would not want to think of themselves as ignoramuses. Later, in his autobiography, Trotsky skimped this part of his youthful experience – revolutionists do not care to remember their Bar Mitzvahs. Towards the end of his life Trotsky showed an unexpected flicker of interest in 'the Jewish question', but now, in early youth, he entered eagerly upon that total abandonment of 'Jewishness' which was itself becoming a tradition among Jewish revolutionists in Russia.

A bright and high-minded boy, young Bronstein was shaken by the misery he witnessed among the peasants. There are stories of quarrels with his father over the mistreatment of peasants, recollections of the boy's quick shame at seeing a peasant woman wait mutely all day long for a word from the elder Bronstein. Once, seeing the father bully a peasant, the boy ran home to his bed and 'oblivious to everything, I sobbed away in spite of my standing as a second-year [school] boy'.

At the age of ten he was sent off to Odessa where he boarded with a cultivated relative, Moissei Spentzer. Here the boy touched the rim of the world of serious conversation, books, music, and the arts. A Southern port famous for its easy-going cosmopolitanism, Odessa possessed a fairly liberal intelligentsia, some of whom visited the Spentzer home. There too the boy learned the pleasures of wandering about in a good library. 'I developed a fondness for Italian opera which was the pride of Odessa . . . I even did some tutoring to earn money for theatre tickets.

For several months I was mutely in love with the colora-
tura soprano . . . who seemed to me to have descended
straight from heaven to the stage boards of Odessa.' One
recalls a brilliant story by Isaac Babel, also about a
Jewish boy infatuated with an opera singer in Odessa. The
groundwork was being laid here for Trotsky's life-long feeling that 'authors, journalists and artists stood for a world
more attractive than any other, open to the elect'. Odessa
helped make him, perhaps more than any other Russian
revolutionist of his generation, into a man of the West.

Cultural awakening and social conscience often emerge
together. Discovering books and opera, the boy also joined
a demonstration at school against a teacher who had
tormented another student simply because he was of
German descent. Young Bronstein was suspended for a
year; it was the kind of incident that in a free society
may be passed off as trivial but that in Tsarist Russia
could shape a man's character, even his history. Back in
school, the boy felt a heightened sense of his individual
powers, a new responsiveness to the claims of others, a
grasp of how events can test the resources of character.
In his autobiography Trotsky looked back with a notable
intensity upon this incident:

> Such was my first political test, as it were. The class was
> henceforth divided into three distinct groups: the tale-
> bearers and envious on one side, the frank and courageous
> boys on the other, and the neutral and vacillating mass in
> the middle. These three groups never quite disappeared even
> in later years.

That the boy saw his schoolmates in quite so defined a
way hardly seems credible; but no matter. For the passage
is typical of the mature Trotsky, typical of a style of
thought not always congruent with his professed system of
thought. Regarding himself as an orthodox Marxist, he
would always insist that moral criteria could not be
formed, or understood, apart from the decisive influences
of historical circumstances. Yet in this passage – as if
projecting backward upon his boyhood the sense he had

of the varying moral compositions of the Bolshevik leaders during the 1920s, those who caved in before the Stalinist bureaucracy and the 'frank and courageous' ones who held true to Bolshevik principles – he speaks of his classmates through the language of traditional valuations of character. And he would do the same throughout his life, employing moral criteria by no means simply derived from or reducible to class interest. He would speak of honour, courage and truth as if these were known constants, for somewhere in the orthodox Marxist there survived a streak of nineteenth-century Russian ethicism, earnest and romantic.

To complete his education, young Bronstein left in 1896 for the town of Nikolayev. In this provincial city, just acquiring the rudiments of modern industry and a modern proletariat, he made his first acquaintance with socialist ideas. A circle of students and workers used to meet in the hut of a gardener to discuss radical ideas, and soon Bronstein's was a leading voice among them. Like any number of other Jewish boys in Eastern Europe, he was very bright; but we ought not to suppose that he came to his mature political opinions instantaneously or without hesitations. At first he spoke of himself as a partisan of Russian populism, a somewhat sentimental creed celebrating the virtues of 'the people' and attacking 'Marxist dogmatism'. At one meeting of this little group in December 1896 he raised his glass in challenge to a young woman of Marxist persuasion and cried out angrily: 'A curse upon all Marxists, and upon those who want to bring dryness and hardness into all the relations of life!'

Is it an indulgence of retrospect to think that Trotsky was already starting to experience within himself a struggle that would last his entire life, a struggle between the side of him that yielded to 'dryness and hardness', indeed, revelled in the stern clamourings of authoritarian command, and another side that came out sometimes in his writings on culture and literature and most forcefully when he found himself in political opposition? At any rate, the object of his attack, Alexandra Sokolovskaya, grew understandably outraged and fled the meeting, vowing to have nothing more to do with this uncouth young man. But both her arguments and her person had made a stronger impression on him than he allowed himself to admit. In a short while, he was converted to Marxism and to Sokolov-skaya; she became his first wife and throughout the years remained a loyal political colleague.

At the age of eighteen, in the tradition of self-sacrifice established by the Russian radicals of the nineteenth century, Lev Davidovich Bronstein chose the life of a professional revolutionist. From this decision he never turned back, though few men in our century have suffered so acutely for having made it. What such a life could mean has been eloquently described by Edmund Wilson : 'Forced to pledge for their conviction their careers and their lives, brought by the movement into contact with all classes of people, driven to settle in foreign countries whose languages they readily mastered – these men and women combined an unusual range of culture with an unusual range of social experience . . .'

Nor was Bronstein's a mere academic decision. In the spring of 1897 his little group began to form a clandestine organization, the South Russian Workers Union, which held political discussions and issued leaflets attacking conditions in the local factories. The writing and hectographing, at the rate of two hours a page, was done by Bronstein himself. Green and untrained, the group naturally made mistakes; the police soon closed in to arrest most of its members. Some were flogged. Bronstein was kept for several months in lice-ridden solitary confinement. Transferred to an Odessa prison, he remained there for a year and a half, and then was sentenced to four years in Siberia.

Settled now along the Lena River, beyond the Arctic Circle, the young revolutionist found himself in a place where all was 'dark and repressed, utterly remote from the world'. By comparison with later concentration and labour camps that would be located in Siberia, Trotsky's banishment was child's play. He used his time to study the Marxist classics, hold discussions with other exiled comrades, sharpen his mind, and strengthen both body and character. In Siberia he read copies of the Social Democratic paper *Iskra* (*The Spark*) and Lenin's pamphlet *What Is To Be Done?* in which the future leader of Bolshevism argued that only by creating a highly disciplined and centralized party staffed by full-time professional revolutionists, a party moving sharply away from the practice of the European Socialists, could the Russian revolutionists survive the persecution of the Tsarist police.

In his Siberian exile Trotsky found himself sufficiently self-assured as a publicist, and untroubled as a 'convict', to write essays on a range of social and literary topics, some of them for a liberal paper in Irkutsk. Among his literary subjects were Ibsen, Zola and Gogol, and three-quarters of a century later these pieces by a young man in his twenties still bear the aroma of talent. They are marred by postures of bravado, that excess of assurance Marxism can give new converts, and also by lush phrasing. But they show the rarest of literary gifts: the ability to observe a scene or read a text carefully. In a piece about life in the Siberian villages there crops up a sentence of the kind that marks the true writer: 'In thoughtful silence our village is dying from disease.' In another essay he writes: 'The spiritual estate of man is so enormous and so inexhaustible in its diversity, only he who stands on the shoulders of great predecessors can claim originality' – not itself an original idea but interesting as an anticipation of *Literature and Revolution* and other texts in which Trotsky insists, against some of his Marxist colleagues, that even through the most volcanic of revolutions the continuity of human culture matters. Or again: 'The purpose of art . . . is not to copy reality in empirical detail but to throw light on the complex content of life by singling out its typical features.' Good for any critic at any time, this remark is especially good for a young man strongly influenced by the Russian essayists of the nineteenth century and the newly emerging Russian Marxists, both of whom were inclined to minimize the autonomy of art and bring a lumbering social utilitarianism to their consideration of novels and poems.

Politics was Trotsky's main interest during the time of his exile, and politics, for Russian revolutionists of that moment, necessarily meant, first of all, 'the organizational question'. The question, in turn, meant primarily what kind of revolution, and thereby revolutionary movement, was possible in Tsarist Russia; what perspective might the radicals bring to bear upon a backward autocracy that, though in a few cities it shared some characteristics of capitalism, was clearly a society with problems sharply different from those the European Social Democrats were trying to confront. To outsiders, Marxist polemics often seem hopelessly obscure, and sometimes they are precisely that; but just as often, behind the scrim of jargon, questions of great importance are being debated. The 'organization question' agitating a few thousand people in Siberia and European exile would affect the future not only of Russia but of the entire world.

Most of the major Russian Marxists were now living as exiles in Western Europe, making the first efforts towards establishing an all-Russian Social Democratic party. This required, first of all, tighter relations than had previously existed between the émigrés and the scattered illegal or semi-legal groups in Russia. Feeling that he was stuck away in Siberian exile and eager to meet, learn from, and no doubt impress such Marxist theoreticians abroad as George Plekhanov, Julius Martov, and V. I. Lenin, Bronstein escaped from Siberia in the autumn of 1902, apparently without great difficulty. He secretly made his way across Russia, and taking the name of a jailer as the 'party name' by which the world would come to know him – a curious choice offering possibilities for amateur psychoanalysis – Bronstein, now Trotsky, smuggled himself across the frontier and headed for London.

There he made straight for the house of Lenin, a man in his early thirties yet already regarded as a 'veteran' of the movement. The two revolutionists took long walks through the streets of the city, an alien city, as Lenin kept suggesting, a city that belonged to 'them'. This implication, Trotsky later recalled, 'was not in the least emphasized, but coming as it did from the very innermost depths of the man, and expressed more by the tone of his voice than by anything else, was always present . . . To his eyes, the invisible shadow of the ruling classes always overlay the whole of human culture – a shadow that was as real to him as daylight.' That the shadow was real made all the more urgent their conversations about the underground movement in Russia and the difficulties of shaping it into a coherent party.

For the old-timers among the émigrés – famous or once-famous names like Plekhanov, Vera Zasulich, Martov – the young Trotsky seemed to be something of a problem. He was talented, enormously talented. The warm-hearted Zasulich adopted him as a protégé, declaring him to be 'undoubtedly a genius'. Martov, future leader of Menshevism and himself a gifted publicist, remarked that Trotsky's literary works 'reveal indubitable talent . . . and already he wields great influence here thanks to his uncommon oratorical gifts . . . He possesses knowledge and works hard to increase it.' Marvellously young, alive with zeal, intellectually quick, Trotsky – or 'the Pen', as he came to be known – seemed to the exiles an incarnation of that political élan they hoped would stimulate their movement. Yet something about him was troubling, perhaps his virtuosity, perhaps his vanity, perhaps his aggressive individuality. Plekhanov, the intellectual eminence of Russian Marxism, took an immediate, open dislike to Trotsky. Distinguished men don't always enjoy encounters with youthful disciples, for they are experienced enough to notice the snake of competitiveness as it twines itself round the branches of admiration. Plekhanov, a witty and cosmopolitan intellectual, detected in Trotsky some of his own least admirable traits: literary vanity and imperiousness of manner.

Lenin was more objective, more coolly impersonal. He saw Trotsky as a valuable recruit to the slender phalanx of revolutionary exiles and, what for him came almost to the same thing, as a political ally in the factional disputes reaching a climax among the editors of *Iskra*. Trotsky began contributing to the paper articles full of revolutionary fire, but also characterized by what Lenin (in a letter to the other editors recommending Trotsky's appointment to their board) nicely called 'traces of the feuilleton style'. Hardly, for Lenin, a compliment. Trotsky, added Lenin, 'accepts "corrections" in silence (and not very readily).' It makes a piquant scene: the great stylist of a few years later, master of a terse aphoristic prose, stands with bitten tongue before Lenin, accepting (not very readily) slashes in his rhetoric.

Still, Trotsky profited from his training among the émigrés, absorbing from them the traditions of Russian radicalism and entering into the differences of outlook that were threatening their unity. They sent him on a lecture trip to Paris, where he impressed the revolutionary groups with his eloquence and eagerness. There, in Paris, the young Trotsky experienced two major encounters: first, with Western art, and second, with a charming young Russian named Natalya Sedova who was to become his second wife and remain with him to the last day of his life.

There were still elements of the provincial in Trotsky. He told Sedova that Paris 'resembles Odessa, but Odessa is better'. Sedova, in a memoir she later wrote, brushed this sentence aside as 'absurd', and Trotsky himself, in his autobiography, said about this dismissal: 'Yes, it was just like that.' For

I was entering the atmosphere of a world centre with an obstinate and antagonistic attitude . . . It was a case of a barbarian struggling for self-preservation. I felt that in order to get close to Paris and understand it fully, I would have to spend a great deal of mental energy. But I had my own world of revolution, and this was very exacting and brooked no rivals . . . In point of fact, I was resisting art as I had resisted revolution earlier 'in life, and later, Marxism; as I had resisted, for several years, Lenin and his methods . . . It was only during my second exile from Russia [after the 1905 revolution] that I came closer to art – saw things, read, and even wrote a little about it.

Experiences of this kind, though they played a greater

part in Trotsky's life than he would later acknowledge, had to be put aside once he became caught up with the internal discussions and disputes of the revolutionary émigrés. By the time the Second Congress of the Russian Social Democratic Party (really the first, since the earlier one had been inconsequential) was held in 1903, Trotsky was a figure of some importance in his little world. He refused to align himself completely with either of the factions then coming into existence, the Bolsheviks (majority) of Lenin or the Mensheviks (minority) led by Martov. In historical retrospect, this division can be seen as an anticipation of the great split that came to its conclusion during the First World War between the revolutionary and reformist wings of the socialist movement; but at the time the issues were still murky, the leaders still uncertain, and even a sympathetic observer might have been excused for supposing that the two groups were indulging themselves in the arid scholasticism that has always been a curse of émigré radicals. Disinclined – he supposed by conviction, but we might add by temper – to tie himself to any party apparatus, and tending to oscillate unsteadily from one side to the other, Trotsky succeeded in provoking the distrust of almost all his comrades.

At stake was a bit of phrasing as to who might be considered a member of the newly formed party: someone who 'personally participates in one of its organizations' (Lenin) or someone prepared to 'co-operate personally and regularly under the guidance of one of the organizations' (Martov). How little the exact wording mattered is indicated by the fact that a few years later Martov would subscribe to Lenin's formula. Nevertheless, the differences between the two groups would soon be of enormous consequence.

In his book *What Is To Be Done?* Lenin had advanced the view that the forthcoming revolutionary party in Russia must be one of severe discipline, strict centralism, hierarchic structure, and consist of a corps of 'professional revolutionists' who would devote themselves entirely to the work of the party. Forcefully, cogently, he wrote:

I assert: (1) That no movement can be durable without a stable organization of leaders to maintain continuity; (2) that the more widely the masses are drawn into the struggle and form the basis of the movement, the more it is necessary to have such an organization and the more stable it must be; (3) that the organization must consist chiefly of persons engaged in revolution as a profession; (4) that in a country with a despotic government, the more we *restrict* the membership of this organization to those who are engaged in revolution as a profession . . . the more difficult it will be to catch the organization; and (5) the *wider* will be the circle of men and women of the working class or of other classes of society able to join the movement and perform active work in it.

This view of party organization derived, in part, from a keen evaluation of the special conditions under which a revolutionary movement would have to be built in Tsarist Russia, a country hardly enabling the creation of a mass, legal party devoted to public education and parliamentary activity. As Lenin remarked caustically at the Congress: 'When most of our activities have to be confined to limited, secret circles and even to private meetings, it is extremely difficult, almost impossible in fact, for us to distinguish those who only talk from those who do the work.' But Lenin's view also followed from a strong belief that the party of revolution had to share some of the traits of an army, to be prepared for combat, and thereby to be radically different from the loose and sprawling parties – Social Democratic included – of the West. A major problem in the study of Bolshevism has been to determine the relative weights to give, or to decide which relative weights Lenin wanted to give, to the distinctively Russian determinants of this theory of party organization and the claim that it held for all kinds of societies.

What happened at the Second Congress was that a group of highly intelligent men struggled to find out what it was they believed. There was little conscious dissimulation; there was much confusion, uncertainty and hesitation to drive opinion towards an extreme. On the face of it, Lenin's view does not seem nearly so terrible as critics later made it out to be. For what is so undemocratic about insisting that 'personal participation' be required from members of a party? How can one suppose that in this or any other phrase there is to be found, as historians have suggested, the kernel of Bolshevik authoritarianism?

If none of the delegates could possibly have supposed that the subtle difference in phrasing between Lenin and Martov prepared for the deadly clash between Communism and Social Democracy of a few decades later, they nonetheless showed, on all sides, a sharp awareness that what they *felt* to be at stake was extremely important. The veteran Axelrod asked, 'Is not Lenin dreaming of the administrative subordination of an entire party to a few guardians of doctrine?' In reply to this keen question Lenin insisted that under the circumstances imposed by Tsarism centralization of decision-making was necessary and, indeed, could only take place abroad, where the leaders could work freely, as they could not in the underground. The party could not afford to be heterogeneous in ideology, for then it would not be able to act decisively and would fail in its central task of raising the workers to socialist consciousness. Lenin was proposing, in effect, what has come to be known in the Marxist vocabulary as a 'vanguard party' – small, compact, highly disciplined, totally dedicated. A tremendous weight was thereby placed on the intellectuals, a body of militant theorists cut off from the normal pursuits of society, transforming itself into a sort of monastic secular order that would speak to and for the working class but necessarily would be apart from it. Whatever else, Lenin's conception was much clearer than Martov's, since it had the virtue of entailing a good deal of realism with regard to the immediate situation in Russia; but Lenin did not, could not yet have grasped the enormous implications of what he was proposing, certainly not the elevation of 'the party' to a kind of monitor of history before which the will of its participants had to be subdued.

In this dispute Trotsky sided with Markov. He argued that the Leninist model of a conspiratorial party ran counter to the Marxist premise that the liberation of the working class must occur mainly through its own conscious efforts. In a report he later wrote about the Congress, he attacked Lenin for his 'iron fist' and charged that Lenin was trying to transform the 'modest' party centre into 'an omnipotent Committee of Public Safety'. A year or two later Rosa Luxemburg, the great Polish revolutionist, would join in the attack on Lenin: 'Nothing will more surely enslave a young labour movement to an intellectual elite hungry for power than this bureaucratic straitjacket, which will immobilize the movement and turn it into an automaton manipulated by a Central Committee.' Trotsky explicitly, and Luxemburg implicitly, had in mind a comparison with the Jacobins during the French Revolution who, while speaking in the name of the people, established themselves as an elite corps of revolutionists acting apart from the people.

Soon after the Congress, Trotsky issued a pamphlet, *Our Political Tasks*, bringing together his criticisms of Lenin. He denounced Lenin for elevating the revolutionary intellectuals to a status presumably superior to that of the working class; he noticed the dangers of creating an 'orthodox theocracy' at the top of the party; he shrewdly anticipated the dangers of 'substitution', by means of which a self-appointed vanguard comes to suppose that it *is* the class in whose name it speaks and for which it makes sacrifices. Instead, Trotsky advanced a concept of party organization fairly close to that of Rosa Luxemburg, who at about the same time was writing: 'The party must seek the guarantee of its stability in its own base, in an active and self-reliant proletariat, and not in its top caucus . . .'

It would be a mistake to dismiss these polemics as the musty remains of European Marxism, if only because the same or similar issues continue to be debated to this day in many kinds of political movements. And even those who are impatient with the history of Russian radicalism may be familiar with a sentence Trotsky wrote at this point, since it invariably appears in studies of the Russian revolution as well as anti-Bolshevik arguments. 'Lenin's methods', wrote Trotsky, 'lead to this: the party

organization at first substitutes itself for the party as a
whole; then the Central Committee substitutes itself for
the organization; and finally a single "dictator" substitutes
himself for the Central Committee.'

This remark is striking, of course, for its anticipation
of the process of degeneration that was to overtake the
Bolshevik party during the 1920s, yet one may doubt that it
is quite so prescient as some historians have supposed.
Certainly it is not sufficient evidence for the claim that in
his youth Trotsky grasped the causes of the decline of the
Bolshevik Revolution in a way that the older Trotsky
refused to acknowledge. For while touching upon an aspect
of Bolshevism that has certainly been open to grave criticism, Trotsky's remark does not, nor could it possibly be
expected to, disclose the complex causes of that degeneration. Any effort to explain a major historical development,
such as the rise of Stalinism, through the workings of an
exclusive cause, such as the Leninist doctrine of organization, is likely to prove superficial.

What is valid in the attacks that Trotsky and Luxemburg made upon Lenin's views regarding party organization, should by now be utterly clear. The 'vanguard party'
tends to equate itself too easily with the class it claims
to be representing; it assumes a homogeneity of interest
and outlook in that class which is rarely present, and
thereby it dismisses the claims of other radical parties to
be authentic representatives of the working class or
portions of it. Yet these· tendencies towards political
usurpation hardly exhaust the complex actuality of the
Bolshevik party during the years when Lenin was its active
leader. Lenin did not, it should be stressed, rule out debate
within his party; in fact, at least until the early or mid-
1920s, the Bolshevik movement was characterized by a
remarkable openness, indeed ferocity, of internal debate.
Factions were frequently set up as formal groups; divergent
bulletins of opinion were issued within the party, and
sometimes factional newspapers appeared in public. At
some points this compares rather favourably with the
records of the European Social Democratic parties, among

whom bureaucratic practice has not been exactly un-
known.

Still, while the internal liveliness of the Bolshevik party
under Lenin constitutes a sufficient ground for distinguish-
ing it from the Stalinist and post-Stalinist varieties of
European and Asian Communism, it is not an adequate
reply to the more nuanced criticisms that can be made of
the Leninist outlook. The Bolshevik tendency to regard
the party as a kind of 'chosen' instrument of history; to
dismiss other socialist parties as 'petty bourgeois' or even
'counter revolutionary'; to invest party loyalty with an
aura of consecrated righteousness; to make of the 'correct
party line' a shibboleth of piety; to 'elevate' practices and
structures required by special Russian conditions into
universals supposedly holding for all capitalist countries –
all these created a complex of attitudes intolerant of the
atmosphere in which a democratic polity must be
grounded. That the Bolsheviks could and did debate freely
with *one another* does not yet mean they were prepared
to accept the norms and limitations by means of which
competing opinions survive in a democracy.

Later, when he identified himself with Leninist orthodoxy, Trotsky naturally minimized the importance of his
youthful attacks on Lenin's organizational views. Or he
would acknowledge, with a candour infrequent among
political ideologues, that he had been wrong. But simply to
accept either the young or the mature Trotsky as correct or
incorrect, simply to pit the views of one against the other,
is to lose some of the complexity and difficulty that
his career displayed. It is not quite a matter of the 'soft'
Trotsky against the 'hard' Trotsky, the semi-Menshevik
against the semi-Bolshevik, though there is some warrant
for such a contrast. Nor is it simply a matter of a
'Western' Trotsky, drawn to the freedoms of intellectual
life, against the 'Russian' Trotsky, driven to a harsh politics
by the circumstances of his country. The oscillations,
indecisions and uncertainties in Trotsky's pre-1917 views
regarding party organization may profitably be seen as a
reflection of an inner struggle within the entire Marxist

tradition, and especially its Bolshevik wing, between democratic, fraternal, even utopian impulses and what are taken
to be authoritarian necessities imposed by the struggle for
power. At various points in his career, Trotsky verged
sharply in one or the other direction, yet never quite gave
up the portion of his mind or sensibility he felt obliged
to suppress for the moment. This was one of the reasons
many Old Bolshevik *apparatchiks* never felt at ease with
him; he could be at least as ruthless as they during the
hard years of the Civil War, yet what were they to make
of a Bolshevik leader who suddenly took two weeks off
to write about literature and speak in defence of at least a
partial artistic autonomy?

Though siding with the Mensheviks in party organization, Trotsky began, in the early years of the century, to
express views on another fundamental problem – the
relationship in the coming Russian Revolution between the
socialists and the liberal bourgeois parties – that brought
him closer to Lenin. Since, as all Russian Marxists agreed,
the first task was to overthrow the Tsarist regime and
establish a government that would initiate democratic
rights – that is, in the Marxist vocabulary, 'complete the
bourgeois revolution' – the Mensheviks argued that the
liberal bourgeoisie would have to take the lead and the
working class serve as a loyal opposition. Trotsky, by
contrast, insisted that the socialists should keep a clear
distance from the bourgeois parties and not compromise
with liberalism. Not yet clear on all points, this position
formed the embryo of his later 'theory of permanent
revolution'.

These discussions, apparently so academic, soon involved
the destinies of millions of people. For the moment, however, they were happily put aside when the Russian people,
long voiceless and dormant, began in 1905 to stir against
the Tsarist tyranny. In Petersburg a demonstration led by
an orthodox priest, Father Gapon, called for democratic
rights; the Tsar ordered his troops to fire into the crowd.
From Geneva Trotsky wrote in a state of high excitement:

One day of revolution was enough, one magnificent contact between the Tsar and the people was enough for the idea of constitutional monarchy to become fantastic, doctrinaire, and disgusting. The priest Gapon rose with his idea of the monarch against the real monarch. But, as behind him there stood not monarchist liberals but revolutionary proletarians, this limited 'insurrection' immediately manifested its rebellious content in barricade fighting and in the outcry: Down with the Tsar! The real monarch has destroyed the idea of the monarch . . . The revolution has come and she has put an end to our political childhood.

Throughout the year 1905 Russia was in a turmoil of rebellion. Strikes closed the factories, street demonstrations broke out in the cities, the crew of the warship *Potemkin* mutinied. One of the first exiles to return to Petersburg, Trotsky for a time lived a political life that was half-public, half-clandestine. Belonging to neither the Menshevik nor Bolshevik faction, but contributing frequently to the press of both and acting with a boldness neither could match, Trotsky became the popular tribune of the revolutionary left. In October there met in the capital the Soviet of Workers' Delegates, a kind of rump parliament of representatives from the unions, left parties, and popular organizations, in which Trotsky soon rose to the post of chairman. Unlike the Bolsheviks, who until Lenin's arrival in November were sceptical about the Soviet because they feared it would threaten their political identity and claims to revolutionary supremacy, Trotsky grasped the enormous potential of this new, spontaneous organ of political action. His personal fearlessness, his combination of firm political ends with tactical ingenuity, and his incomparable gifts as an orator helped to transform him, at the age of twenty-six, into a leader of the first rank: he had entered upon the stage of modern history and only the axe of a murderer would remove him. Here is a passage from one of his speeches before the Soviet, a characteristic flare of virtuosity, in which he tells about a conversation with a liberal who had urged him to moderation:

I recalled to him an incident from the French Revolution, when the Convention voted that 'the French people will not parley with the enemy on their own territory'. One of the members of the Convention interrupted: 'Have you signed a pact with victory?' They answered him: 'No, we have signed a pact with death.' Comrades, when the liberal bourgeoisie, as if boasting of its treachery, tells us: 'You are alone. Do you think you can go on fighting without us? Have you signed a pact with victory?' we throw our answer in their face: 'No, we have signed a pact with death.'

In the fifty days of its existence the Soviet experienced the dilemma frequently faced by revolutionary institutions: it was strong enough to frighten the government but not strong enough to overthrow it. Finally, Tsarism regained the initiative, for it was not yet so fully discredited as it would be in 1917 and the revolutionary movements were still unripe and inexperienced. In the repressions that followed, thousands were killed and imprisoned; reaction once again held Russia. Together with the other leaders of the Soviet, Trotsky faced public trial, at the climax of which – for now he stood firm in the sense of his powers, secure in the knowledge that he had established himself in the line of the great European rebels, convinced that he had found the key to history – he made a brilliant, openly defiant speech:

A rising of the masses is not made, gentlemen the judges. It makes itself of its own accord. It is the result of social relations and conditions and not of a scheme drawn up on paper. A popular insurrection cannot be staged. It can only be foreseen. For reasons that were as little dependent on us as on Tsardom, an open conflict has become inevitable . . . no matter how important weapons may be, it is not in them, gentlemen the judges, that great power resides. No! Not the ability of the masses to kill others, but their great readiness themselves to die, this secures in the last instance the victory of the popular uprising . . .

Again Siberia : this time deportation 'for life'. But it was a saving feature of pre-totalitarian despotisms that they were often inefficient, so that even before reaching his Arctic destination Trotsky could make a superbly bold escape, being driven by a vodka-besotted peasant for a whole week through ferocious blizzards and across the frozen tundra.

For the young Marxist who only a few months earlier had been sentenced to Siberia 'for life', the escape was a personal triumph : in retrospect one might say, a personal triumph with historic portents. But now that he was safe again in Europe, Trotsky turned back to his pen, composing his first major work, *1905*, a historical study that in scope and vigour anticipates the *History of the Russian Revolution*.

Though not so commanding in structure or rich in detail as the *History*, *1905* is a distinguished piece of historical writing – especially when one remembers that its author was under thirty when he wrote its somewhat disparate segments. *1905* lacks the sustained narrative line of the *History*, it does not venture upon the ambitious theoretical generalizations of the *History*, and only occasionally can it compare for vividness in the portraiture of major actors. Yet, at some points, *1905* seems to have a reliability as record of events that is more persuasive than that of the *History*. It is not so completely at the mercy of a grand ideological scheme as the later book, nor so thoroughly subservient to the unfolding of a supposed historical progress. Event and interpretation are here somewhat ill at ease with one another, and precisely this roughness of execution, this occasional uncertainty and hesitation, lends *1905* a convincing air of verisimilitude.

Though in *1905* a short-breathed writer, Trotsky is admirably close to his materials, in touch with the swirl and chaos of the events he describes. The narrative rises and breaks; there are gaps in both story and idea; no Marxist enclosure or completion is possible with regard to a sequence of events still betraying uncertainty, inexperience, improvisation. Perhaps another way of saying this is that Trotsky does not here feel obliged to deal with the vexing problem of the relation between the Bolshevik party and the upsurge of the masses. The Bolsheviks played only a minor role in 1905 and Trotsky was by no means inclined to give them an inch more of credit than he had to. Instead of a schema of purposeful, indeed, almost inevitable revolution that controls the latter portion of the *History*, we find here elemental confrontations between an obtuse, sluggish oligarchy and masses of people suddenly thrust into political consciousness, testing for the first time the pleasures of opinion and speech. There is no 'guiding hand', firm or shaky, from a 'vanguard party'. There is only the improvised legislature of the masses, the Soviet or council, through which they seek coherence and legitimacy.

Trotsky's prose in *1905* is fresh, lucid and, like all his historical works, remarkably free of Marxist jargon. The 'feuilleton style' about which Lenin had complained is all but gone; the writer bows to his subject, finds his language through submitting to the momentum of fact. Occasionally he allows himself terms of insult and contempt when talking about the autocracy, terms he will no longer need in the *History*; for now, in the years after 1905, the autocracy still rules, and with a heavy fist, while after 1917 it will be no more than a pitiable relic. Elements of his later style are also present : the sardonic, gleaming passion, the eye searching out dramatic or revealingly incongruous moments (as in an astonishing vignette about his visit to a nobleman's home where he is to lecture before a group of aristocratic officers).

Politically the greatest strength of *1905* lies not in its by now familiar rehearsal of the theory of permanent revolution, but in Trotsky's stress – not nearly so evident in the *History* – upon the overwhelming, almost supra-class absolutism of the Tsarist state :

> Absolutism reached the apex of its power when the bourgeoisie, having hoisted itself on the shoulders of the third estate, became sufficiently strong to serve as the adequate counterweight to the forces of feudal society. The situation in which the privileged and owning classes, by fighting one

another, balanced one another, ensured maximum independence for the state organization. Louis XIV was able to say '*L'état, c'est moi.*' The absolute monarchy of Prussia appeared to Hegel as an end in itself, as the materialization of the idea of the state as such.

In its endeavour to create a centralized state apparatus, Tsarism was obliged not so much to oppose the claims of the privileged estates as to fight the barbarity, poverty, and general disjointedness of a country whose separate parts led wholly independent economic lives. It was not the equilibrium of the economically dominant classes, as in the West, but their weakness which made Russian bureaucratic autocracy a self-contained organization. In this respect Tsarism represents an intermediate form between European absolutism and Asian despotism, being, possibly, closer to the latter of these two.

Whether or not deliberately, Trotsky was here picking up a strand of Marx's thought – the Marx who wrote that in Louis Napoleon's France the state' takes on a kind of independent life, 'is an appalling parasitic body, which enmeshes the body of French society like a net and chokes all its pores'. The view that the state can be not merely an agency acting on behalf of a ruling class but also, and sometimes still more so, an independent body weighing heavily upon all of society – this view, so important to twentieth-century political thought, was not to be stressed by the classical Marxists. Trotsky turned to it in 1905 because he was seeking to explain the special features of Tsarist autocracy; later he devoted considerably less attention to this matter, not seeing sufficiently that the power of statist absolutism in Russia has been a phenomenon overarching particular modes of class rule and persisting, in fact, as a veritable constant of its backwardness.

These were hard times for the Russian revolutionists. The Tsar took a merciless revenge as he cut away a great many popular rights. In Russia the socialist movements came close to collapse from police harassment and inner demoralization, while in exile they kept fragmenting into embittered factions. Trotsky continued vainly to urge that the Bolsheviks and Mensheviks reunite: perhaps he did not fully grasp the extent of their disagreements, perhaps he feared what the consequence of grasping it might be. Wandering from country to country, often after being expelled by the police, and earning a bare living through political journalism, he found himself in New York during the war years, and there he wrote for a radical Russian paper until word of the March 1917 revolution brought him rushing back to his homeland. During the years between the two Russian revolutions Trotsky's main intellectual work was the development – and defence against critics within the movement – of his theory of permanent revolution, a bold set of speculations concerning Marxist strategy in backward countries:

1) Tsarist Russia is a backward country in which the immediate task is the bourgeois-democratic revolution that will confront those problems which, historically, have been solved by the great bourgeois revolutions of the past: such problems as the overthrow of the autocracy, the abolition of semi-feudal relations in the countryside, the right to self-determination for oppressed national minorities, the convocation of a constituent assembly to establish a republic, the proclamation of democratic liberties, etc. Because of the traditional backwardness of Russia and its need to defend vast land masses against invaders, there arose a highly centralized and powerful state autocracy. 'Even capitalism appeared as the child of the state' – that is, the scattered centres of capitalist development in Tsarist Russia, far from arising in opposition to the despotic restraints of the government, were intimately connected with and dependent upon the bureaucratic autocracy of Tsarism.

2) The 'task of the bourgeois revolution', however, must be accomplished in Russia long after the bourgeoisie as a class has lost the revolutionary élan of its youth. Because of the special backwardness and isolation of Russian society, the Russian bourgeoisie is characterized by timidity and indecision. It has many social and economic reasons for opposing the Tsarist autocracy, yet is bound to it by links of petty interest, prestige and cowardice. Above all,

it shares with the autocracy a growing fear of the two main classes at the base of Russian society: the peasantry and the workers. In developing this point Trotsky was fond of quoting a sentence from Peter Struve, an ex-Marxist writer: 'The farther we go to the east in Europe, the more slavish, cowardly and mean is the political conduct of the bourgeoisie.' Because of these congenital weaknesses, the Russian bourgeoisie is incapable of a revolutionary initiative even on behalf of its own interests; it cannot make 'its own' revolution. Consequently the tasks of the bourgeois revolution in a backward country like Russia must now be fulfilled by the plebeian classes. Or, to put forward a seeming paradox, the bourgeois revolution has partly to be made against the bourgeoisie.

3) While it rests with the working class and the peasantry to carry through the bourgeois revolution, these classes are not socially or historically of equal weight. The peasantry – because of its geographical dispersion, centuries-long passivity, tradition of petty ownership, and lack of common outlook – has shown itself incapable of taking the historical lead. Its role has always been to serve as a crucial but subordinate ally of an urban class.

4) The sole urban ally now available to the peasantry – unless it remain the collective serf of Tsarism – is the proletariat. For Trotsky the inevitable conclusion is that the bourgeois-democratic revolution can be completed in a backward country only under the leadership of the working class, small and inexperienced though it may be – which means, more particularly, only under the leadership of the revolutionary party speaking for the working class. But the workers, having gained power, will not be able to stop short before the problems of the bourgeois revolution. The very effort to cope with these will inevitably force them to go beyond the limits of bourgeois property, so that, as Trotsky wrote later, 'the democratic revolution grows over immediately into the socialist, and thereby becomes a *permanent* revolution'.

5) The socialist revolution thus begun in a backward country cannot be completed within national limits, since the economic base is not sufficiently secure nor the working

class sufficiently strong and conscious. Power could be held and steps towards socialism taken only if there speedily followed victorious revolutions in the advanced European countries. Russia's very backwardness would thrust her forward in the revolutionary scale and bring her under the rule of the working class, perhaps before any of those countries which, because of their economic maturity, were commonly regarded as most ripe for socialism. But this same backwardness, after having forced the working class to power, would overtake it and drag it down unless it received aid from abroad. Or as Trotsky later put it: 'In a country where the proletariat has power . . . as the result of the democratic revolution, the subsequent fate of the dictatorship and socialism is not only and not so much dependent in the final analysis upon the national productive forces, as it is upon the development of the international socialist revolution.'

Unquestionably this was the boldest theory, the most extreme prognosis, advanced by any Russian Marxist in the years before the First World War. The full measure of its audacity can be grasped even today by anyone who troubles to break past the special barriers of the Marxist vocabulary and examine the theory in terms of the tensions between 'underdeveloped' and advanced countries in the twentieth century. The vexing problem of the relation between backwardness and industrialization, which today preoccupies all serious political thinkers, was to be solved, as Trotsky saw it, by the historical audacity of the barely developed proletariat in the colonial countries. For the Mensheviks, who believed that the bourgeoisie would have to lead the forthcoming bourgeois revolution, Trotsky's theory was an absurdity. Even Martov, the most original of the Menshevik theorists, wrote: 'We have the right to expect that sober political calculation will prompt our bourgeois democracy to act in the same way in which, in the past century, bourgeois democracy acted in western Europe, under the inspiration of revolutionary romanticism.' Martov did not sufficiently consider, it now seems clear, how limited a 'revolutionary romanticism' must be if it must act under the prompting of 'sober political calculation'. Lenin, though agreeing with Trotsky as to the historical impotence of the Russian bourgeoisie, felt that the Russian working class was still too weak and inexperienced to play the grandiose role assigned to it by Trotsky and that the revolution would have to be carried through by an alliance between proletariat and peasantry, the exact relationship between whom he refused to specify or predict. The idea of a revolutionary government replacing Tsarism and yoking bourgeois and socialist objectives seemed implausible to Lenin for reasons at once historically limited and historically prescient: 'This cannot be, because only such a revolutionary dictatorship can have any stability . . . as is based on a great majority of the people. The Russian proletariat constitutes now a minority of Russia's population.' Later, after the Russian Revolution, Lenin tacitly acknowledged the prescience of Trotsky's theory, and in retrospect it seems no exaggeration to add that of all the Marxists it was Trotsky who best foresaw the course of events in Russia.

But not entirely. Precisely the brilliance of Trotsky's historical prognosis enables us, decades later, to see its inherent weaknesses. The grand over-all strategy of a world-historical transformation led by an aroused and increasingly self-confident working class which takes upon itself the 'mission' assigned to it by Marxism – this prognosis has not been realized, nor does there seem at the moment much reason to expect its realization, at least in any form that Trotsky would have acknowledged, either in the advanced or underdeveloped nations. Other classes, or social formations aspiring to the privileges and powers of an ascendant class, have brushed the proletariat aside or subordinated it to ends that clash with Marxist expectations. The 'hegemony' of the working class which is the beginning and the end of Trotsky's theory proves increasingly questionable: in the Western countries because the working class becomes subject to the social constraints and accepts both the advantages and 'rules' of the welfare state, and in the underdeveloped countries because the working class proves to be relatively weak and unassertive.

Whether these facts – and facts they are – call into question the entire Marxist schema regarding the role of the working class in the building of socialism and thereby the possibilities for a socialism resting on the autonomous, democratic efforts of the working class: this remains a question that must haunt every thoughtful socialist. Suffice it to note that even the modest strainings among segments of the European Social Democracy to move beyond the present limits of the welfare state do not give much support to Trotsky's theory.

Like most revolutionary Marxists, Trotsky did not foresee the extent to which the working class in the industrialized countries would choose to act within the parliamentary system as the way to achieve its aims. Workers with homes, cars, television sets are not likely to yield to insurrectionary visions, unless, perhaps, they are suddenly and drastically deprived of the benefits they have won through their unions and political parties. Expectations, or desires, for such an apocalypse persist among the tiny groups of Trotskyist faithful and other orthodox Marxists, but that it will come is at least doubtful and that it would necessarily enable a turn towards socialism still more so.

If, then, we look back to the particularities of the Russian situation, we must conclude that the help from a victorious European proletariat that Trotsky hoped would salvage the Russian Revolution was not to be forthcoming – nor, in broader terms, was help to be forthcoming to the underdeveloped countries of Asia, Africa and Latin America in sufficient quantities to forestall the brands of authoritarian dictatorship that would flourish there. In this negative sense, Trotsky was extremely prescient: deny adequate help from the industrialized West, which he insisted could come only through a victorious proletariat, and the social development of the underdeveloped countries must necessarily take distorted, almost certainly authoritarian forms.[1]

Trotsky tended also to overestimate the capacity of the proletariat in the underdeveloped countries – a proletariat likely to be concentrated in a few industrial centres like

Shanghai or Bombay – to take upon itself the role of national leadership. In his vision of things, the working class of such a country, small and young though it might be, would come to the forefront in the struggle against foreign domination, push through those internal reforms that Marxists had designated as pertaining to the 'bourgeois revolution' (a republic, division of the land, political rights, etc.) and then proceed boldly to a leap across both centuries of backwardness and the capitalist phase of historical development. This course would be made possible through an alliance with the victorious working class of the West.

That, in fact, the bourgeoisie of these underdeveloped countries, dependent on foreign capital and lacking a strong dedication to national purposes, would fail to realize its own 'historical tasks' – this part of Trotsky's theory has been all but entirely vindicated by experience. He, and not the Mensheviks, nor even Lenin, has been proven right on this point. There cannot be, has not been, and never will be a smooth, gradual entry of the underdeveloped countries into the historical phase of bourgeois industrialism that, in effect, would repeat the development of the West. That the bourgeois revolution would now have to be completed without the leadership of, and often in direct opposition to, the bourgeoisie of the underdeveloped nations – this has been shown to be a reality of our time. But what Trotsky quite failed to see was that there were other possibilities, beyond the spectrum of Marxist expectation (or any other of his time). In some countries, like China and Vietnam, the revolution for national independence and against imperialist domination would be completed not under the leadership of the working class but by an insurgent elite of nationalist intellectuals, declassed semi-intellectuals, and party bureaucrats using the symbols and vocabulary of Communism in order to establish its authoritarian power. This elite would find far more support in the countryside than among the urban proletariat.[2]

The tasks of 'modernization', a fashionable term that in recent political discussion has replaced 'the bourgeois revolution, have in fact been undertaken by neither of the classes Trotsky assumed to be decisive: neither the bourgeoisie nor the proletariat. Those tasks have been undertaken by authoritarian bureaucracies rising to power 'above' classes – above the insecure or exhausted proletariat, above the supine peasantry, above the dispersed bourgeoisie. The society thus established could call large numbers of people into political motion, but rarely, if ever, grant them the right to an autonomous or critical politics. It would be neither capitalist nor, in any traditional sense envisaged by Marxists, socialist. Bringing together the most up-to-date methods of propaganda and the repressive habits of Byzantine state bureaucracies, these regimes would attempt, seldom with much success, to drag their nations into the modern world, using brute force, militarized radicalism, primitive exploitation. Perhaps what is being said here is simply that Trotsky failed to anticipate the modern phenomenon of the totalitarian or authoritarian state, which would bring some of the features of permanent revolution into a socio-economic development having some of the features of permanent counter-revolution. Nevertheless, even in its weakness or errors, Trotsky's theory remains a valuable lens for seeing what has happened in the twentieth century – but a lens that needs correction.

2   The Seizure of Power

During the feverish months of 1917 politics seemed to grip the whole of Russia. Theories long debated among the revolutionists in exile were now determining the political strategies of major parties. What the emigres had been squabbling about in 1903 or 1906 proved to be of immediate practical consequence.

The scoffers, the jokers, the 'realists' for whom the antics of left-wing theoreticians had been a subject of mockery – it was *they* who proved ill equipped to deal with the new Russia. The right-wing groups were hopeless: they dreamed of restoring the Tsar, the whip, the nobleman, the priest. The bourgeois liberal Kadets who now took power in the Provisional Government failed to understand that the revolution spreading across Russia was an elemental social upheaval, not to be wrenched to an abrupt halt at some point of convenience. Most of the political tendencies on the left acted in accord with the ideas they had spent years in developing. The populist Social Revolutionists (SRs) were, as always, sincere, romantic, confused, divided – some of them authentic figures out of the Russian depths unable to deal with Russia's deepest problems. The Mensheviks, who by now had brought to completion the classical virtues and weaknesses of Social Democracy, held to the view that the revolution would necessarily be unable to go beyond the limits of a bourgeois revolution since backward Russia was 'not ripe for socialism'. (A formula at once perceptive and scholastic: as if history always proceeds by fixed or appropriate stages, obedient to the commands of the possible!) Trotsky and his small group of friends, now participating in a left-socialist group called the *Mezhrayontsi*, regarded the events of 1917 as a vindication of the theory of permanent revolution – and up to a point they were right in seeing those events as a popular upsurge overflowing the limits of a bourgeois revolution'. Only

Lenin showed enough flexibility to shake off some of his earlier ideas and undertake a rapid strategic shift. Between April and October 1917 he steadily approached the position of Trotsky.

Trotsky himself had spent the war years first in Europe and then, briefly, in New York working as a journalist and participating in the affairs of left-wing socialist groups. With the outbreak of the February 1917 revolution, which swept away the Tsar and for the first time in history brought democratic liberties to Russia, Trotsky made his way back to Petersburg, eager to share in the decisions and excitement of Russian politics. The February revolution had come as a great popular explosion, almost spontaneous in character (though in his *History of the Russian Revolution* Trotsky argued that locally, in the proletarian districts of Petrograd and Moscow, the revolution had often been guided by experienced rank-and-file revolutionists, many of them Bolsheviks). Now, in the spring of 1917, a long-mute nation was learning the rudiments of public speech. Intoxicated with its freedoms, the people of the major cities threw themselves into debates and demonstrations; newspapers were started, parties launched; and for the radicals it seemed as if, through some blessing of history, everything they had been waiting for was finally at hand.

Within Russia the situation was desperate: defeat in war, an army all but shattered, an economy badly disrupted, chaos in many parts of the countryside, no clearly established or universally accepted institutions of authority. The February revolution had brought into existence two major, and competing, centres of power: the Provisional Government and the Soviets. At first the Provisional Government drew largely upon the constitutional monarchists and the Kadets, and then, as the mood of the people grew more radical, it shifted towards the moderate socialists. As for the Soviets, they were improvised representative bodies or 'parliaments' of workers and soldiers, and dominated at the start by the Mensheviks and SRs.[1]

The Provisional Governments, headed successively by Prince Lvov, the Kadet Miliukov, and the populist Kerensky, were inherently unstable. Their class base was weak, uncertain; they were often inefficient, perhaps unavoidably so; there was little experience, either at the top or the bottom of the nation, in the ways of democracy; and both on the right, among the regathering monarchist officers, and on the left, among the growing cadres of the Bolsheviks, powerful enemies were waiting to destroy the young democracy. Still more important was the incapacity or unwillingness of all the provisional governments to undertake a division of the landed estates among the peasants and bring to an end the fruitless, exhausting war. Russia might make war or it might experience revolution; it could not do both at the same time. Mainly for ideological reasons but also out of the timidity that often besets liberals and social democrats upon taking office, the Provisional Governments failed to satisfy the desires of the people. Month after month, despite leftward shufflings of personnel, these governments became increasingly isolated.[2] Once great expectations are aroused during times of revolutionary upheaval, moderate parties can rarely satisfy the masses – this is one of the premises of Trotsky's theory of permanent revolution and it was an insight that allowed him to conclude that the revolution was not to be confined according to some formula. Lenin, a far better political strategist than Trotsky, quickly worked his way towards the same grasp of things.

Since Trotsky opposed political collaboration with the Provisional Governments, even when they included representatives of the moderate socialist parties under the flamboyant Kerensky, he found himself increasingly at odds with the Mensheviks. And, for a while, with the Bolsheviks too. During the first few months of 1917 the Bolshevik group in Petersburg was under the leadership of a 'conciliationist' wing which advanced a perspective not radically different from that of the Mensheviks. (There was even talk of a reunification of the two movements.) This 'conciliationist' leadership, consisting of party veterans who had not gone into exile but had provided the leading cadres within Russia, sought to bring pressure on the Provisional Governments on behalf of popular demands, tried to strengthen its representation within the Soviets, spoke of an all-Soviet government, but clearly had not the slightest thought of either an insurrection to be undertaken by the Bolsheviks outside the Soviets or the exclusive assumption of power by the Bolsheviks through the Soviets. This leadership was following the line of the old Lenin, the Lenin who had put forward the theory of 'the democratic dictatorship of the workers and peasants'. But once Lenin came back to Russia in the spring of 1917, he quickly rebuked the resident leadership for its 'conciliationist' policy and in his famous 'April theses' advanced a sharply new perspective – fierce attacks on the Provisional Government, no collaboration with the Mensheviks or other moderate socialists, popular agitation for 'land, bread and peace'. The question of power remained muffled, but those with keen political ears could hear it in the throb of Lenin's speeches.

What did the taking of power mean to Lenin at this point? In the spring of 1917 he was still proposing the formation of a Soviet government – 'all power to the Soviets: a government made up of SRs and Mensheviks and responsible to the Soviets . . . At this moment but only at this moment . . . this kind of government can take power by peaceful means . . .' So wrote Lenin, and so, for some months, he continued to write. But the moderate socialists, petrified in their doctrines, refused 'on principle' to take office by themselves, without the liberal bourgeois parties as their partners – though it seems beyond question that they could have done so, peacefully and with popular backing. As late as September 1917 Lenin was writing that by taking power 'the Soviets could still – and this is probably their last chance – ensure the peaceful progress of the revolution'. His opponents would later charge that all this was merely a ruse, a device for deflecting attention from the Bolshevik plans for insurrection; but the probability seems, if we follow the most recent and sophisticated historians of the revolution, that while more certain in his mind than most of his Bolshevik colleagues, Lenin did for a time genuinely oscillate between the idea of a Soviet government and a Bolshevik seizure of power. In any case, the crucial point politically is that despite the growing radical moods of the masses, the Mensheviks and SRs never took up the challenge by trying to form an all-socialist government. Only a small minority of left Mensheviks, led by the brilliant and touching Julius Martov, spoke for such a government. Most of his comrades, however, turned to this idea only after the Bolsheviks had taken power, and then it was too late.

Without a formal acknowledgement – politics rarely yields them – Lenin had begun to fill out his algebraic formula, 'the democratic dictatorship of the workers and peasants', with the arithmetical content of Trotsky's 'permanent revolution'. Insofar as he did so, Lenin moved from the idea of a Soviet government to the plan for a Bolshevik insurrection (though the matter was to be complicated by the fact that the Bolsheviks would win a majority in the Petrograd Soviet and launch their insurrection in its name). It was only natural that by July 1917 Trotsky and his friends should formally join Lenin's party and take within it posts of high responsibility.

Working closely with a disciplined party organization for the first time in his career, Trotsky now became the popular spokesman for Bolshevism during the months of revolutionary ferment and upheaval. The gifted Menshevik Sukhanov, whose eyewitness account of the Russian Revolution is a major historical source, has recalled that Trotsky 'spoke everywhere simultaneously. Every worker and soldier at Petrograd knew him and listened to him. His influence on the masses and the leaders alike was overwhelming.' In his autobiography Trotsky left a striking description of his role as revolutionary orator:

I usually spoke in the Circus in the evening, sometimes quite late at night. My audience was composed of workers, soldiers, hard-working mothers, street urchins – the oppressed under-dogs of the capital. Every square inch was filled, every human body compressed to its limit. Young boys sat on their fathers' shoulders; infants were at their mothers' breasts. No one smoked. The balconies threatened to fall under the excessive weight of human bodies. I made my way to the platform through a narrow human trench, sometimes I was borne overhead. The air, intense with breathing and waiting, fairly exploded with shouts and with the passionate yells peculiar to the Modern Circus. Above and around me was a press of elbows, chests, and heads. I spoke from out of a warm cavern of human bodies; whenever I stretched out my hands I would touch someone, and a grateful movement in response would give me to understand that I was not to worry about it, not to break off my speech, but keep on. No speaker, no matter how exhausted, could resist the electric tension of that impassioned human throng. They wanted to know, to understand, to find their way. At times it seemed as if I felt, with my lips, the stern inquisitiveness of this crowd that had become merged into a single whole. Then all the arguments and words thought out in advance would break and recede under the imperative pressure of sympathy, and other words, other arguments, utterly unexpected by the orator but needed by these people, would emerge in full array from my subconsciousness. On such occasions I felt as if I were listening to the speaker from the outside, trying to keep pace with his ideas, afraid that, like a somnambulist, he might fall off the edge of the roof at the sound of my conscious reasoning . . .

Leaving the Modern Circus was even more difficult than entering it. The crowd was unwilling to break up its new-found unity; it would refuse to disperse. In a semi-consciousness of exhaustion, I had to float on countless arms above the heads of the people, to reach the exit. Sometimes I would recognize among them the faces of my two daughters, who lived nearby with their mother. The elder was sixteen, the younger fifteen. I would barely manage to beckon to them, in answer to their excited glances, or to press their warm hands on the way out, before the crowd would separate us again . . .

Trotsky was more than a superb orator, more than a sensitive medium between the aroused masses and the straining Bolshevik leadership. In the Soviets, where conflicts among the left-wing parties took their sharpest form, he became the main spokesman for Bolshevism, earning the dislike, even hatred, of many opponents because of what they saw as the polemical ruthlessness and arrogance of his style.

There now followed the 'July days', an outburst of impassioned but undisciplined popular demonstrations. Barely held in check by the Bolsheviks, who feared a premature attempt to grasp power, the 'July days' led to a reaction on the part of the government, including a crackdown on the Bolshevik leadership. Trotsky spent some weeks in prison, Lenin fled into hiding. In August the right wing went into action, undertaking a coup under General Kornilov; but the massed strength of the Petrograd working class, together with crucial segments of the Petrograd garrison, beat back Kornilov's troops. Soviet agitators sent to meet the rebels were remarkably effective in 'melting' their ranks. The coup collapsed, the Bolsheviks gained politically since they had played a crucial role in mobilizing the masses; and the political balance shifted rapidly towards the left. In late September the Bolsheviks won a majority in the Petrograd Soviet, with Trotsky, just out of prison, becoming its chairman. His speech of acceptance contains some sentences which in retrospect bear a tragic import:

> We are certain that the work of the new Presidium will be accompanied by a new rise in the development of the revolution. We belong to different parties and have our own work to conduct, but in directing the work of the Petrograd Soviet we will observe the individual rights and complete freedom of all factions; the arm of the Presidium will never be used to stifle a minority.

Control of the Petrograd Soviet, probably the strongest in the country, gave the Bolsheviks a measure of legal cover for their insurrection – a fairly modest, loosely co-ordinated action which, with little difficulty and only a small amount of blood, toppled the Kerensky government. 'All the work of practical organization of the insurrection' – wrote Joseph Stalin shortly afterward – 'was conducted under the immediate leadership of the President of the Petrograd Soviet,

Comrade Trotsky. It is possible to declare with certainty that the swift passing of the [Petrograd] garrison to the side of the Soviet, and the bold execution of the work of the Military Revolutionary Committee [the body directing the insurrection], the party owes principally and first of all to Comrade Trotsky.' In the government now formed under Lenin, Trotsky became foreign minister. Before we glance at Trotsky's career as international spokesman and military commander of the Bolshevik regime, we must stop to consider the character and meaning of the October revolution itself. For any estimate of Trotsky's role in modern history depends in good measure on what one makes of this revolution.

Two overpowering myths have dominated Western thought about the October revolution. The first is that of the Bolsheviks, celebrating the revolution as the fulfilment of an irresistible upsurge of the masses, a brilliant realization of the historical process as it ushers in the era of socialist revolution – all under the guidance of the expert Bolshevik vanguard. The second is that of anti-Bolsheviks, which deplores the revolution as the work of a small, conspiratorial minority usurping the power of an unstable Russian democracy and thereby initiating those repressions that would characterize Communist totalitarianism in our century. By contrast, I wish to advance the view that, while both of these positions contain elements of truth, each is a grandiose simplification. The closer one comes to the actual events of October 1917, the less one is persuaded of their 'inevitability' in either the Marxist or any non-Marxist sense, and the more one discovers error, weakness, accident, failure and missed opportunities. For certain orders of mind, the claims of historical determinism are always captivating: they foreclose alternatives, banish doubts, yield the comforts of necessity. But the truth is usually more elusive and complicated.

All through 1917 the Bolshevik party kept growing, especially in the major industrial and commercial cities. The reasons for this growth we have already noticed: the difficulties of life in a defeated country, the incapacity of the Provisional Governments to satisfy the basic needs of the people, the ideological rigidity and political flaccidity of the moderate socialists, the frequent skill of Bolshevik agitation and, not least of all, the temptation of a people suddenly released from the bondage of Tsarism to rush towards extreme solutions. Tens of thousands of new members poured into the Bolshevik party, so that the earlier Leninist model of a small, tightly disciplined vanguard had to be modified. Within the party there were now many currents of opinion and these spoke openly, organized themselves as loose 'tendencies', and fought one another sharply. There were also divisions among the party's various organizational segments. In a first-rate study, *The Bolsheviks Come to Power*, Alexander Rabinowitch has shown that during the crucial months of 1917 there were severe conflicts within the party between the Central Committee and the Petrograd Committee, as well as between the party leadership and the Military Revolutionary Committee (set up as an agency of the Petrograd Soviet but actually under Bolshevik control).

The party was badly split between those, like Lenin and Trotsky, who were committed to a perspective of insurrection, and those 'right Bolsheviks', like Kamenev, Rykov, Zinoviev and Nogin, all members of the Central Committee, who favoured continued work within the Soviets and forming a coalition of left-wing parties to replace Kerensky's inept Provisional Government. Had it not been for the overwhelming personal authority that Lenin wielded within the Bolshevik leadership and his persistent demand that it move towards insurrection or face the prospect of an open factional battle – in short, had it not been for the decisive historical role of Lenin, the Bolshevik party would probably not have undertaken the October insurrection. By its very nature, such an assertion cannot be proved; but the evidence seems extremely persuasive. Trotsky has said as much in his *History*, intent upon showing that many of the old Bolsheviks buckled in a moment of crisis and were less close to Lenin's views than he, Trotsky, a newcomer to the inner circle of the Bolshevik leadership. From Rabinowitch we learn that a significant portion of the Bolshevik leadership was dubious about the insurrection, almost certainly a larger portion than actually voted against Lenin.

For the masses of workers and soldiers in the major cities, what seemed desirable – and what their representatives called for – was a *Soviet* government. That meant a government made up of the various left-wing parties, drawing its legitimacy from the growing strength and stability of the Soviets, committed to a wide range of reforms (division of the land, negotiations for peace, an end to capital punishment at the front, 'workers' control' of production, etc.) and the rapid convocation of a Constituent Assembly in order formally to decide the future form of Russian governance. All the evidence accumulated by historians of various opinions seems decisive on this point. In fact, when the Bolsheviks did seize power, they took considerable pains to cloak their insurrection in the protective garments of 'Soviet legality' – though in reality they presented the Soviets with a *fait accompli*, as Lenin candidly kept insisting they must.

Take as an example of a politically sophisticated Soviet the one established in Kronstadt, a naval centre near Petrograd, famous for its independent-minded sailors. The political expectations in this centre of radicalism were obviously different – sharply different – from what the Bolshevik insurrection actually brought into being. The Kronstadt Soviet proposed 'a decisive rupture', writes Rabinowitch, 'with the capitalists; the transfer of power into the hands of the revolutionary workers, peasants, and soldiers; and the creation of a democratic republic'. In this projected Soviet government all socialist groups would participate – though here major difficulties had to be anticipated, not least of all the problem of how to reconcile those who wished to continue the war and those who wished to end it.

There were at least two versions afloat of such a Soviet government: all the non-Bolshevik parties participating, with the Bolsheviks forming a more-or-less loyal opposition, or all parties, not excluding the Bolsheviks, participating so that there would be a considerable tilt leftward.

Complicated negotiations were under way among the left parties. Within the Menshevik party, which had steadily been losing popular support, a left wing led by Martov kept growing stronger. Martov's group agreed with the Bolsheviks in wanting a quick end to the war and a series of immediate reforms which, while short of 'socialism', would certainly push the revolution beyond those 'bourgeois' limits to which in theory the Mensheviks still clung. Among the 'right Bolsheviks' there was sentiment favouring such a coalition regime, since it seemed a way out of the fatality of insurrection – an 'adventure', as Kamenev and Zinoviev saw it, that could well lead to disaster. (A few Bolsheviks foresaw that success might lead to still greater disaster.)

Within the Bolshevik ranks Kamenev and Zinoviev led the group of leaders opposed to insurrection. For many years afterward, this lapse from Leninist orthodoxy would be thrown up to them in the intra-Bolshevik disputes; today, what they said often seems wise. Necessarily they couched their objections to Lenin's perspective in tactical terms, stressing the difficulties and risks of insurrection, as well as the high cost of failure; but it is not hard to discern beneath the surface of their polemic a recognition that the problems of the Bolsheviks would be most severe if in fact they did seize power. In a statement presented to the Central Committee on the eve of October, Zinoviev and Kamenev stressed the importance of the 'petty bourgeoisie' or, as we would say, the middle class. The Russian working class could not itself, they argued, complete the revolution – that is, reach the socialist goals proclaimed by the party. 'We simply cannot lose sight of the fact that between us and the bourgeoisie there is an enormous third camp, that of the petty bourgeoisie. This camp joined with us during the Kornilov affair and brought us victory. It will ally itself with us again more than once . . . but for the time being it is closer to the bourgeoisie than to us.'

Kamenev and Zinoviev were also sceptical of Lenin's claim (did even Lenin really believe it?) that a majority of the Russian population now backed the Bolsheviks. In their view, a majority of the Russian working class and 'a

significant percentage' of the soldiers were with the Bolsheviks, 'but everything else is questionable'. The elections
to the Constituent Assembly, they predicted accurately,
would find the Bolsheviks in a minority, well behind the
peasant-backed SRs. And as for Lenin's claim that 'the
majority of the international proletariat is, allegedly,
already with us . . . unfortunately, this is not so. The revolt
in the German navy has immense symptomatic significance
. . . But it is a far cry from that to any sort of active
support of the proletarian revolution in Russia . . . It is
extremely harmful to overestimate [our] forces.'

Tactically, as it turned out, Kamenev and Zinoviev were
wrong. The seizure of power proved to be rather easy, and
all of the cautions expressed by the 'moderate' Bolsheviks
came to seem unwarranted. But if one transposes these
objections on to a larger historical scale – what it would
cost the Bolsheviks to *keep* power, what it would cost the
Russian people if the Bolsheviks kept power – then the
argument made by Kamenev and Zinoviev has great force.
The middle class, especially the middle peasants in the
Russian countryside, would indeed turn out to be a heavy
weight on the regime. The working class would prove
insufficiently strong or self-assured to maintain a true
socialist morale, or to prevent its political dispossession
by the Bolshevik autocracy. And the international proletariat – here a remark by Trotsky in the course of a polemic
against Martov in 1917 is crucial: 'Were Russia to stand
all on her own in the world, then Martov's reasoning [that
Russia was not yet ripe for socialism] would be correct.'

Still more powerful, indeed prescient, was a statement
made by another moderate Bolshevik, Nogin, a figure about
whom we do not know very much. After the party had
taken power, the question of a coalition government was
raised once more, and when the dominant leadership
insisted upon an exclusively Bolshevik government, Nogin
and several others resigned from the Central Committee.
'Such a government', he said, 'can be kept in power only
by means of political terror.' It would, he continued, signify
an 'irresponsible regime', and would 'eliminate the mass
organizations of the proletariat from leadership in political

life'. These memorable phrases, from a second-rank Bolshevik leader, may serve as underpinning to the arguments of Zinoviev and Kamenev, and perhaps also as an answer to the question asked by Lenin, rhetorically to be sure, in his pamphlet, *Will the Bolsheviks Retain State Power?* – If 130,000 landowners had been able to govern Russia after the 1905 revolution, why could not the 240,000 members of the Bolshevik party govern it now? (One is tempted to remark, the 240,000 could govern but only insofar as they approached and then exceeded the repressive spirit of the 130,000 they replaced.)

The perspective of the 'right' or moderate Bolsheviks was, in short, very close to that proposed by Martov: a parliamentary course premised on the peaceful formation of a Soviet government that, in turn, would prepare for a Constituent Assembly in which the left-wing parties were certain to have a majority and through which they could then authenticate their power democratically. It is only fair to add that the arguments of Lenin and Trotsky against this course had a certain weight. How could one expect Mensheviks and SRs to enact the necessary reforms when, during their months in the Provisional Governments, they had done little or nothing towards that end? How could an all-socialist coalition government take a clear stand on the war when the socialist parties were hopelessly divided? And would not such a regime necessarily be feeble and inconsequent, leading to further demoralization among the people and then the probable victory of a resurgent counter-revolutionary right? There were answers, of course. The anti-war group within the Mensheviks was becoming stronger; pressure from the representatives of the masses would force the all-socialist government into a firmer posture; so strong was the support of the workers and soldiers for the Soviet parties, there was little possibility of a triumphant counter-revolution. We are dealing here with hypotheses, speculations, counter-factuals, and it will never be possible to reach entirely binding conclusions. Yet, as one looks back upon the historical sequel to the Bolshevik seizure of power, it is hard to believe that the fate of Russia would have been worse had the party followed the line of Zinoviev, Kamenev, Nogin and the other 'moderates'. It is just barely possible that Russia would then have kept to a democratic course. Here, if anywhere, is an answer to the question of the role of the individual in history: Lenin's overmastering authority and political gifts, his decision to press for insurrection, were crucial.[3]

During the weeks immediately after the seizure of power, all the differences of opinion among both the Bolsheviks and the ousted left-wing parties were sharpened to a point of fury. A series of confrontations occurred in which the principal actors sensed that far more was at stake than the immediate issues in dispute:

— Mid-day, 25 October. The insurrection in Petrograd has triumphed, the Petrograd Soviet convenes. Trotsky announces: 'On behalf of the Military Revolutionary Committee, I declare that the Provisional Government no longer exists!' Excitement, applause. Need anyone trouble to remember that only a day earlier Trotsky had said that an armed conflict 'today or tomorrow, on the eve of the [All-Russian] Congress [of Soviets] is not in our plans'? A voice cries out from the floor: 'You are anticipating the will of the Second Congress of Soviets!' And Trotsky, aflame with revolutionary confidence, cries back: 'The will of the Second Congress of Soviets has already been pre-determined by the fact of the workers' and soldiers' uprising.' Through this appropriation of the will of the workers and soldiers, the triumphant Bolsheviks make certain that the Soviets can have no independent will.

— That same evening the All-Russian Congress of Soviets convenes. The Bolsheviks command an absolute majority, evidence that indeed they have made deep inroads among the masses. (By July the Bolshevik party in Petrograd numbered 32,000 members; the Mensheviks 3000.) At the Congress the right SRs and Mensheviks launch a fierce denunciation of the Bolshevik seizure of power: it is a violation of democratic norms, it undermines Soviet

legality. Martov, speaking for his small group of left
Mensheviks, proposes that the Congress undertake a peaceful resolution of the conflict with an eye towards creating
an all-Soviet government preliminary to the Constituent
Assembly. The delegates applaud. Lunacharsky, a 'moderate' Bolshevik, rises to say that his party 'has absolutely
nothing against the proposal made by Martov'. Is this
spoken in sincerity? For some Bolsheviks, apparently so;
for others, it is a tactical device to buy time with which
to consolidate their power. Martov's proposal is passed
unanimously. At this very point the right SRs and Mensheviks, in a grave blunder, choose to walk out of the
Congress, arguing that the issue has already been settled
by guns.⁴ Martov, torn between a desire to condemn the
Bolshevik insurrection and a need to compromise with it,
introduces a resolution attacking the *'coup d'état'* but calling for an 'all democratic' government including the Bolsheviks. At this point Trotsky, the most effective Bolshevik
speaker, moves to the platform, standing close to his old
friend Martov. In the packed hall an American witness,
John Reed, watches Trotsky 'with a pale, cruel face, letting
out his rich voice in cool contempt' as he answers Martov:

> A rising of the masses of the people requires no justifica-
> tion. What has happened is an insurrection, and not a
> conspiracy. We hardened the revolutionary energy of the
> Petrograd workers and soldiers . . . No, here no compromise
> is possible. To those who have left and those who tell us
> to do this, we must say: You are miserable bankrupts, your
> role is played out: go where you belong – to the dustbin
> of history.

From the man who a few years later will himself be
harried into exile, these are sad and terrible words; sad
and terrible in their failure to see that it is not always the
least worthy or even politically 'correct' who end up in
the dustbin of history.

Trembling and helpless, Martov shouts back, 'Then we'll
leave!' His comrade, Boris Nicolaevsky, recalls that Martov
then

walked in silence and did not look back – only at the exit did he stop. A young Bolshevik worker . . . turned on Martov with unconcealed bitterness: 'And we among ourselves had thought, Martov at least will remain with us.' These words stung Martov. He stopped and in a characteristic movement tossed up his head as if making ready to reply but then he said only: 'One day you will understand the crime in which you are taking part.'

That the young Bolshevik worker, Ivan Akulov, will himself disappear in the Stalinist purges of the 1930s – the historical irony is almost too neat, too painful.

– A very faint possibility remains that an all-Soviet government will be formed. In early November the powerful union of railway workers, *Vikzhel*, declares at a session of the Soviet Congress that it remains stubbornly opposed to the seizure of power by one party; it demands the creation of a regime based on all the socialist parties; it declares its intention of keeping control of the railways and threatens, in case of reprisals against its members, to cut off food supplies from Petrograd. Not an idle threat: this is a strategically located union. Negotiations follow: Lenin and Trotsky stall for time; but, as even so intrepid an anti-Bolshevik historian as Leonard Schapiro writes, 'to many other Bolshevik leaders the negotiations appeared as an honest attempt to form a broader coalition and thereby to avert civil war and minority rule by force'. Again, with a painful lack of realism, the right SRs and Mensheviks take a haughty posture, arguing at first that the Bolsheviks must be excluded from such a government because they have violated democratic legality. (No doubt; but they also have the power . . .) Then the right SRs and Mensheviks concede the possibility of a coalition with the Bolsheviks, provided Lenin and Trotsky are excluded from the government. Had the, by now, largely powerless socialist groups deliberately chosen to play into the hands of Lenin and Trotsky, they could hardly have done better. At a subsequent meeting of the Bolshevik Central Committee Lenin says, 'The discussions [initiated by *Vikzhel*] should have been treated as diplomatic cover for military action' – that is, to give the Bolshevik government time to send reinforcements to Moscow, where the insurrection is far from completed. Meanwhile, the split among the Bolsheviks widens. On 15 November prominent 'moderate' Bolsheviks at the Soviet Central Executive Committee vote against the line of their party regarding coalition negotiations. Two days later seven or eight members of the Bolshevik government resign their ministerial posts in protest against the suppression of the liberal bourgeois press. But their revolt soon peters out, partly because the opposition to Lenin within the leadership is not firm or principled enough, partly because the other socialist parties show a staggering ineptitude, and partly because the issue has already been decided. Power rests with Lenin and Trotsky, at least in the capital, and even though a few left SRs enter the government for a time, it is the Bolsheviks who rule. But for a little while, at least, the opposition can still speak: the opposition of dissident radicals. Six weeks after the October insurrection, Maxim Gorky's newspaper, *Novaia Zhizn*, prints a devastating criticism of the new rulers:

Power has passed to the Soviets only on paper, in fiction, not in reality. The Second All-Russian Congress of Soviets faced an accomplished seizure of power by the Bolsheviks, not by the Soviets. The sessions of the Congress proceeded in an atmosphere of insurrection, the Bolsheviks relied on the force of bayonets and guns . . . In the provincial cities, where the Soviets hesitated, where no Bolshevik majority was assured, the Bolsheviks sought to intimidate the Soviets . . . The slogan 'All power to the Soviets' had actually been transformed into the slogan 'All power to a few Bolsheviks'. . . . The Soviets are already losing their effectiveness, the role of the Soviets shrinks to nothing . . . A Soviet republic? Empty words! In reality it is an oligarchic republic, a republic of a few People's Commissars.

Perhaps I have been making too much of the idea of a socialist coalition government – after the October revolution, it must be admitted, little more than a wistful hope. The idea matters not so much in its own right but as a test of the intentions and values of the main political actors. Defenders of Bolshevism wishing to give it a somewhat democratic cast, would later argue that there was nothing inherently undemocratic in the fact that Lenin formed a government composed exclusively of his own party people – this happens in democratic countries repeatedly. True; but the assumption of power by a single party can be regarded as democratic only if it has come to power through democratic means and continues to respect the rights of parties out of power. It is because these conditions were not, or could not, be met by the Bolsheviks that the negotiations into which they entered in late 1917 with the other socialist parties were doomed to fail. Trotsky was right, in a sense, when he taunted Martov by saying that no compromise was possible. Compromise would have meant that a party which had forcibly seized power would be prepared to share it with parties from which it had been seized. That was not perhaps totally impossible, but it was surely most unlikely. It could have occurred only if there had been forces powerful enough in Russia to press the Bolsheviks into taking such a step, which might also have meant forces powerful enough to have thwarted the insurrection in the first place. The 'moderate' Bolsheviks had regrets perhaps, they certainly felt uneasiness and forebodings – but they did not have the moral and intellectual courage to oppose Lenin in the way that, if their view had prevailed in the party, he would have opposed them.

When Lenin had first come to Russia after the February 1917 revolution, he declared that the new Russia was the freest country in Europe. He was right. Public liberties never before experienced in the land of the Tsars, outbursts of political energy held in check for generations, the advance to articulateness and activity of social classes and political groupings long mute, and the development of new social forms such as the Soviets and local peasant committees – these are but a few signs of that freedom. To be sure, in the months between February and October the social problems of the country accumulated, or at least made themselves felt, a good deal faster than they could be solved. To be sure, many of the criticisms made by the far left, both Bolshevik and non-Bolshevik, of the ineptitude and timorousness of the Provisional Governments were accurate. And it seems also likely that the country required some kind of stabilization: the political feverishness characterizing 1917 could not continue indefinitely. Lenin's political intuition led him to recognize that a moment had come – it might, he knew, never come again – in which power could be seized. Trotsky's brilliant oratorical gifts and tactical leadership helped realize Lenin's programme. But within a short time of their success no one could seriously say about Russia what Lenin had said in the spring of 1917: that it was the freest country in Europe.

Trotsky the theoretician was vindicated. The idea of a 'going-over' from bourgeois to proletarian revolution – this provided a grand historical justification for the Bolshevik seizure of power. But it was precisely this same theory that also provided an explanation of why the Russian Revolution, unless quickly rescued by revolution in the West, was bound to collapse or degenerate. Let a minority regime take power in the name of socialism and it would have to employ measures of repression and then self-mutilation that it had not dreamt of – *but that its critics, even then, had warned about.* Let a minority regime take power in the name of socialism and it would have to resort to improvisations, wild oscillations, unforeseen draconian steps in the realm of economic policy that it had not even troubled to consider. For as Sukhanov noted, in all Bolshevik propaganda before the seizure of power, 'no economic programme was even referred to'.

The difficulties that must follow have been noted both by pro- and anti-Bolshevik historians, often in strikingly similar terms. Isaac Deutscher, a partisan of Bolshevism, writes about 1917 and the period immediately following it:

The plebeian democracy of the Soviets [his designation for the Bolshevik regime] did not at first think of itself as a

55

monolithic or totalitarian state because its leaders were confident that the bulk of the Russian people shared their aspirations. It did not soon occur to them to consider what they would do if this hopeful assumption proved wrong.

Keen but a little disingenuous. For all along Martov was raising precisely this question, and so too were the scorned 'conciliationists' inside the Bolshevik party. They were warning that the imperatives of power, wielded by a minority regime that in a disrupted and impoverished society tries to impose radical changes upon a population often suspicious and sometimes deeply resistant, could lead only to repressive dictatorship. No one, of course, quite foresaw the horrors of Stalinism during its worst years, but many people, on the left and elsewhere, saw that conditions were being created that might enable a Stalin to take over. And had not Trotsky himself – the earlier Trotsky – warned of such possibilities?

Flushed with power, magnificent in his gifts and his heroism, Trotsky could now see only the fulfilment of the dream of revolution. He gave no public credence to the possibility that the other part of his earlier self – the Trotsky who had kept warning against Bolshevik mono-lithism and usurpation – might also be proved right. Persuaded that the historical foresight he associated with Marxism had enabled the world-shaking revolution to conquer, he lacked the critical perception, or tragic insight, to suspect that this very foresight might also be linked to historical blindness.

Was there something inherent, some 'original sin' of doctrine or disposition, in the Bolshevik movement that foredoomed the rise of totalitarianism? Or was the reality more complicated and problematic, with authoritarian elements in Bolshevik thought brought into excessive prominence as a result of mistaken decisions, the arrogance of power and historical circumstances that obviously made a democratic path very difficult, no matter who ruled Russia? This is not a question that can be answered with certainty, though I am inclined to believe the second of these variants. The historian Leonard Schapiro, whose book

The Origin of the Communist Autocracy is the most thorough account of the steady destruction of liberties under the Bolshevik regime, takes the view of the Bolsheviks

> that their passion for justice was bound to lead to disaster when once they failed to see the need for reconciling all the conflicting interests which will always exist in practice in every state . . . in a form of stable legal order. Without the restraining *ne plus ultra* of law and independent judges it is very tempting for any government to sacrifice first the majority to a minority, then today to tomorrow, and finally one generation to future generations. This is what Lenin and his successors seem to have done. But they acted as they did, at any rate when they first set out, because they believed that in so doing they were serving the cause of justice.

This seems a just and balanced criticism, far from the crude view that asserts Bolshevism and Stalinism to be indistinguishable or Bolshevism to be totalitarian in 'its essence'.

Since this book is not a history of the Russian Revolution, we need proceed no further with this historical excursus. Suffice it to say that the Constituent Assembly, in which the Bolsheviks had only about 25 per cent of the vote, was forcibly dispersed in January 1918 by the Bolshevik regime, and thereby the last opportunity for a parliamentary democratic course was lost. But what else, come to think of it, could the Bolsheviks have done? How could a regime established through insurrection submit itself to the possibility of check or dismissal by an assembly chosen through popular ballot? Had the Bolsheviks been ready to make that submission, they would not have had any reason to make the revolution.

That at least in the big cities the Bolsheviks had a vast popular following in 1917 and for a little while afterward, seems true. That their insurrection was more than the coup of a conspiratorial minority, seems also true. But none of this is to deny the fact that in their seizure of power the

Bolsheviks violated the fundamental norms of democracy, norms to which at least some of them had an ambivalent attachment. Once, however, even Lenin's critics within the party had condoned or accepted the consequences of the insurrection, they were in a poor position to block its undemocratic consequences.

Embodying the hopes of vast numbers of Russian workers, soldiers and peasants, drawing upon the vibrant idealistic tradition of European socialism, erupting fiercely within the depths of a tormented nation, the October revolution nevertheless created the terms of its own un-doing. On the day the revolution succeeded, it set loose energies of counter-revolution – from within its own flawed premises, from the selflessness of many who fought and died for it. In the light of distance, revolution and counter-revolution come to seem all but inseparable.

3   Bolshevism Overreaches Itself

As foreign minister of the new Bolshevik government, Trotsky intended, as he joked, to issue 'a few revolutionary proclamations and then close shop'. The reality was to be more complicated. He had hastily to improvise a new ministry out of the shambles of the old, and to conduct the difficult Brest-Litovsk negotiations with imperial Germany, which brought peace to Russia at a heavy cost. During these negotiations Trotsky disagreed with Lenin. Lenin proposed that the new government sign a treaty with Germany at almost any price, so urgent did he feel peace to be for Bolshevik survival. Trotsky, hoping for proletarian revolution in Germany, adopted a delaying tactic, punctuated by his astonishing revolutionary speeches before the German representatives at Brest-Litovsk. Within the Bolshevik party a 'left' group led by Nikolai Bukharin advocated a policy of 'revolutionary war' – publishing for a time its own paper and constituting almost a mini-party within the party. The right of public disagreement among the Bolshevik leaders was still taken for granted.

In 1918, when civil war broke out across the whole of Russia, Trotsky became minister of war. He had no military experience behind him, other than the dubious advantage of having served as a journalist during minor warfare in the Balkans. With little but revolutionary principles and revolutionary élan, he quickly created an army out of almost nothing. At his disposal were a few thousand Bolsheviks, members of the party militia, or Red Guard, who had fought in the revolution and could at best be regarded as a paramilitary force; a considerable group of Russian army officers willing to serve the new regime in a non-political capacity; and masses of untrained recruits who lacked discipline and often enough arms.

For almost two years Trotsky lived in an armoured train

which served as the mobile political-military headquarters of the new army. Racing from front to front, working with ferocious energy, exposing himself in crucial battles to rally green or frightened troops, insisting upon the military authority of the old officers while keeping them in check through a network of political commissars, holding fast to standards of efficiency and discipline among soldiers who had long been demoralized, but above all else, stirring his followers to fight and die through the exaltation of his speeches and manifestoes, Trotsky created – not he alone, of course, but he at its head – an army that finally defeated the Whites. He understood that in a revolutionary army it is the will to struggle that is decisive. Victory would come only as the men fighting with him believed themselves to be crusaders for a better world, only as they were ready to face death out of a conviction that they were – to quote from one of Trotsky's speeches to the soldiers – 'participants in an unprecedented historic attempt to create a new society, in which all human relations will be based on . . . co-operation and man will be man's brother, not his enemy'.

The actuality of this 'new society' during the civil war years was very far from brotherliness. It could not have been otherwise. The breakdown of industry, the enormous exertions and sacrifices required by civil war, the blockades and interventions of the capitalist powers, the economic inexperience and mistakes of the Bolsheviks, the growing disaffection of the peasantry (which had wanted the land, but no more), and a partial disintegration of the Russian working class as a result of industrial paralysis, military service and flight from the starving cities – all this could only mean suffering, hunger, death, injustice. Backs against the wall, the Bolsheviks resorted to extreme measures they had never dreamt of in their earlier programmes. Industry was almost completely nationalized. Private trade was banned. Party squads were sent into the countryside to requisition food from the peasants. Wages were sometimes paid in kind, so little value did the government's money have. Politically, all grew more oppressive. The remaining left-wing groups that had tried to strike a balance between supporting the Bolshevik regime and criticizing its excesses, now met with increasing harassment from the Cheka, the newly created secret police.

'War communism', remarks Isaac Deutscher, was a

> travesty of the Marxist vision of the society of the future. That society was to have as its background highly developed and organized productive resources and a superabundance of goods and services . . . [It] was to abolish economic inequality once for all by levelling up the standards of living. War communism had, on the contrary, resulted from social disintegration . . . It did indeed try to abolish inequality; but of necessity it did so by levelling down the standards of living and making poverty universal.

It is from this tragic moment that we have inherited the popular image of Trotsky as a military commander – 'everyone' knows the photograph of him in long military coat, sharp goatee, imperial posture. For the military Bolsheviks, especially those romantics to whom the civil war came to be the central experience of their lives, Trotsky embodied the historical pathos of their cause. For intellectuals throughout the world there was something fascinating about the spectacle of a man of words transforming himself through sheer will into a man of deeds. For the Mensheviks and other defeated left-wing groups still scattered in Russia, Trotsky was perhaps the most hateful of the new rulers: arrogant, harsh, dictatorial, without the nuances of thought or feeling he had shown in his years of exile. And for the *apparatchiks* at the top and middle layers of the party bureaucracy, they who only yesterday had migrated from underground dangers to comforts of power, Trotsky the non-Bolshevik deviant of years past seemed still an interloper. Brilliant but vain, unnerving through his puritanical austerity, too popular to be openly attacked but now and again the butt of vulgar jokes or insinuations, he was never fully accepted into the inner core of the Bolshevik hierarchy.

In the first few years after the revolution Trotsky worked more as leader of the state than leader of the party. He had neither time nor taste for the niceties of bureaucratic caution, and undoubtedly his brusqueness antagonized party officials who a few years later would find means of retaliation. He saw himself as an officer in the army of world revolution who could not be bothered by what was happening in the Organization Bureau of the Bolshevik Central Committee – a rather bad mistake, for in countries with a single party, as even in those with more, what happens in the Organization Bureau can deeply affect basic policy. With Lenin himself, Trotsky's relations were often cordial but rarely close. As the acknowledged leaders of the revolution, the two men worked well together despite frequent disagreements, but some film of memory, imprinted with old attacks and accusations, fell between them.

'Particularly at the beginning', recalls Trotsky's wife,

the occupants of the Kremlin dined more than frugally. Leon Davidovich [Trotsky] used to say, 'We must live no better than we did in exile.' I agreed with him, as I knew very well what privations the workers were suffering. In any case, I was too busy with my job to bother very much about food. The only people who still enjoyed a certain degree of prosperity were the few private businessmen and former property owners who lived off the black market. On one occasion, Trotsky sat down to a meal and noticed some butter. 'Where did that come from?' he asked in astonishment. The secretary of the Central Committee, Leonid Serebriakov, who had been told about our diet by the doctor, had arranged this rare treat for us. It was not until many months later that the members of the government were able to live on an even half-way decent diet.

Perhaps the most vivid portrait we have of Trotsky during the immediate post-revolutionary years comes from Victor Serge, the writer who for a time worked at the centre of the Communist International:

No one ever wore a great destiny with more style. He was forty-one and at the apex of power, popularity, and fame –

leader of the Petrograd masses in two revolutions; creator of the Red Army, which (as Lenin had said to Gorky) he had literally 'conjured out of nothing'; personally the victor of several decisive battles, at Sviazhsk, Kazan, and Pulkovo; the acknowledged organizer of victory in the Civil War . . . He outshone Lenin through his great oratorical talent, through his organizing ability, first with the army, then on the railways, and by his brilliant gifts as a theoretician. As against all this Lenin possessed only the pre-eminence, which was truly quite immense, of having, even from before the Revolution, been the uncontested head of the tiny Bolshevik Party which constituted the real backbone of the State, and whose sectarian temper mistrusted the over-rich, over-fluid mind of the Chairman of the Supreme War Council [Trotsky] . . .

[At a Congress of the Communist International] Trotsky made his appearance dressed in some kind of white uniform, bare of any insignia, with a broad, flat military cap, also in white . . . ; his bearing was superbly martial, with his powerful chest, jet-black beard and hair, and flashing eye-glasses. His attitude was less homely than Lenin's, with something authoritarian about it. That, maybe, is how my friends and I saw him, we critical Communists; we had much admiration for him, but no real love.

In the Bolshevik discussions that now ensued regarding the problems of post-civil war reconstruction, Trotsky's role was at once anomalous and provocative. Like the other major theorists in the Bolshevik camp – Lenin and Bukharin – he was trying to think his way through difficulties no Russian Marxists had quite foreseen, for none had ever imagined anything like War Communism. (Some of their critics had.) In December 1919 Trotsky put forward a series of 'theses' before the party's Central Committee in which he argued for compulsory work and labour armies ruled through military discipline – draconian measures, he admitted, but necessary for lifting the shattered economy to that minimal level of production where ordinary incentives might again begin to operate. Trotsky's scheme had two major objectives: to find a way of bringing back to the factories a dispersed working class and to find a way of employing the energies of the Red Army to rebuild the economy. One premise behind this scheme was that the economy was in so dreadful a condition, only measures of compulsion could be effective at the outset. Another premise, as Trotsky put it, was that 'it is precisely because our technical equipment is worn out . . . that we must increasingly make up for all these shortages with living human energy'.

> It is necessary [he argued] to state openly and frankly in the hearing of the whole country, that our economic condition is a hundred times worse than our military situation ever was . . . Just as we once issued the order, 'Proletarians, to horse!', so now we must raise the cry, 'Proletarians, back to the factory bench! Proletarians, back to production!'

Though supported by Lenin, this proposal encountered stiff resistance from the Bolshevik ranks, especially the trade unionists who were still somewhat responsive to popular pressures and feared the consolidation of a military-bureaucratic elite. For a short while several labour armies were set up and Trotsky would write lyrically, with a striking absence of realism, about their role in 'Communist construction'.

Early in 1920 he underwent a sharp, even traumatic change of mind. During a trip to the Urals his military train was derailed and, despite frantic wireless messages, allowed to remain in the banked snow for many hours. An investigation was set up. It discovered what any casual observer could have described: everywhere a pall of incompetence and apathy, the result of insufficient food, overwork, years of strain. It became clear to Trotsky that, short of large-scale terror, there was no longer much possibility of prodding the masses by means of compulsion, even on behalf of minimal economic ends that, if reached, would have been to their benefit. In a dramatic turnabout, Trotsky now proposed many of the measures that a year later would come to be enacted as the New Economic Policy: an end to requisitioning of crops, the peasants to be allowed to sell their surpluses at a profit, a partial return to the free market. This, jibed some doctrinaire Bolsheviks, was precisely what Menshevik critics had been saying all along.

Trotsky's proposal was summarily defeated. Under Lenin's prompting, the Central Committee hung on to the 'shock measures' of War Communism. What had been begun as a desperate improvisation now came increasingly to be regarded as 'normal' or at least unavoidable. And Trotsky, unfortunately, did not persist in his views. Unwilling to take the issue to the party ranks, fearful that a dispute inside the party so soon after the civil war would have demoralizing effects, Trotsky retreated to his earlier programme of militarized labour and 'shock methods' in economic life. Logic, if not reality, was on his side. It seemed logical to say that, once social relaxation had been rejected, compulsion was the only alternative. But politically this view was disastrous, helping to strengthen all those forces within the party which turned to repressive methods as a way of coping with criticism and discontent.

We witness here, not only in Trotsky himself but in the whole Bolshevik movement, a wild and desperate oscillation with regard to economic policy. The '240,000 Bolsheviks' – by 1920 their actual number had grown to 612,000 – whom Lenin had supposed would be sufficient for ruling the country grow increasingly isolated from the population; they face economic disasters for which they have no clear prescription; they improvise extreme measures involving more and more state bureaucratism on the top and social and psychological exhaustion below. They are paying now – the whole country is paying – for their failure to think through the consequences of their seizure of power.

In the public debates that followed – for a measure of opposition could still be expressed in Russia – the Menshevik leader Raphael Abramovich opposed the labour battalions with the query: 'Wherein does your socialism differ from Egyptian slavery? It was just by similar methods that the Pharaohs built the pyramids, forcing the masses to labour.' Trotsky replied: 'Abramovich sees no difference between the Egyptian regime and our own. He has forgotten the class nature of government . . . It was not the Egyptian peasants who decided through their Soviets to build their pyramids . . . our compulsion is applied by a workers and peasants government.'

An unfortunate argument, Trotsky at his weakest. In advancing it he failed to acknowledge that by 1920 the Russian workers were not deciding very much on their own; it was the Bolshevik government, acting in the name of the workers while often disregarding their desires, that made the decisions. A great deal of the support the Bolsheviks had enjoyed among the workers since the October revolution had been lost. (Deutscher admits: 'If the Bolsheviks had now permitted free elections to the Soviets, they would have almost certainly been swept from power.') The policies of the government could not be justified simply because it called itself a 'workers' government'; its right to that title might better be justified by the kinds of policies it enacted. Most unfortunate of all, Trotsky's argument provided the formula that could later be used all too easily for rationalizing the Stalinist plunge into totalitarianism.

In arguing for the labour armies about which he had privately come to be dubious, and in justifying the oppression of dissident socialist groups, Trotsky invoked the harsh necessity of winning a desperate civil war and salvaging a collapsed economy. As he turned from warfare to economy, working towards the revival of industrial production, all his talents came into play; but his political role took on a harsh authoritarian cast which cannot be justified even to the extent that certain of his measures during the civil war might be. Driven by the force of intolerable circumstances created in part by the Bolsheviks themselves, but also trapped in the vice of a Bolshevik exclusivism which led to greater concentrations of power at the top of the ruling party just when an opening of social and political life might have saved the situation, Trotsky now condoned acts of repression that undercut whatever remnants there still were of 'Soviet democracy'.

Worse yet, he did all this with a kind of excessive zeal, as if to blot out from memory much of what he had said in earlier years.

It was at this time, in 1920, that Trotsky published his book *Terrorism and Communism*, probably the most authoritarian of all his writings. Composed in reply to Karl Kautsky's social democratic critique of the Bolshevik regime, *Terrorism and Communism* breathes the arrogance of the ruler lodged in power, the impatience with liberal refinements of the commander growing accustomed to the grime of civil war, and perhaps a trace of the guilt of the polemicist who, a dozen years earlier, was directing against Lenin arguments not so different from those Kautsky was now launching against him. Yet it must also be said that *Terrorism and Communism* is a powerful work, slashing and clever in its polemical energy.

Trotsky's root idea is that 'history down to now has not thought out any other way of carrying mankind forward than that of setting up always the revolutionary violence of the progressive class against the conservative violence of the outworn classes'. In the bloody civil war between Reds and Whites, preachments about 'the sacredness of human life', the terribleness of Bolshevik methods in the civil war (terrorism, taking hostages, etc.) are either an indulgence of spectators moralizing from a safe distance or mere refusals to acknowledge the imperatives of reality. In his most caustic style Trotsky puts the question to Kautsky:

The bourgeoisie, hurled from power, must be forced to obey [the Soviet state]. In what way? The priests used to terrify people with future penalties. We have no such resources at our disposal. But even the priests' hell never stood alone, but was always bracketed with the material fire of the Holy Inquisition and with the scorpions of the democratic state. Is it possible that Kautsky is leaning to the idea that the bourgeoisie can be held down with the help of the categorical imperative, which in his last writings plays the part of the Holy Ghost? We, for our part, can only promise him our material assistance, if he decides to equip a Kantian humanitarian mission to the realms of [the White Guardists] Denikin and Kolchak.

Once Trotsky is granted his premise – that the politics of the Bolshevik regime are essentially an unavoidable response to civil war, that civil war allows no niceties of choice as to methods, that the use of violence and terror by both sides does not warrant a curse of general dismissal but must be judged according to the social character of the contending forces – once all this is granted, then the argument seems very strong indeed. But what Trotsky does not stop to ask himself is whether these premises must be fully accepted and without question.

Might not criticism from non-Bolshevik radicals supporting the Leninist regime against the White Guards prove useful, as a check upon error and the abuse of power? Were there not impulses towards authoritarianism in Bolshevik practice apart from those stimulated by the civil war? Is political debate to be suspended in a time of civil war? (Trotsky did not think so later on, when he kept urging his policies during the Spanish Civil War.) If indeed the Russian masses were as fervently devoted to the Bolshevik side as Trotsky claims, did this not allow at least some interplay of political life even in the most difficult circumstances? Granted that civil war imposes harsh necessities – not least, the necessity to kill people – should not those who claim to represent a more humane future find it desirable at least to reflect upon the permissibility of certain methods? Are there not some codes of restraint that hold even in extreme circumstances – codes one does not expect a Denikin or a Kolchak to care about but which might concern a Lenin and a Trotsky, if only, perhaps, as signs of the historical-moral superiority of the 'progressive' side? And is there not a danger that the triumphant vindication of detestable methods will prove to be a rationale for their permanent employment?

Such questions can, no doubt, be rendered more complex or subtle, but perhaps it is just as well to keep them in a state of initial simplicity. Complex or simple, they do not seem to have troubled Trotsky when he was writing *Terrorism and Communism*. Anyone familiar with the voice that dominates this book can quickly imagine the scorn with which he would meet such 'petty bourgeois scruples'. Yet Trotsky's argument also reveals itself as very simple, and in a less attractive way than Kautsky's attack. Finally, all that Trotsky is saying comes down to a claim that 'we' in power represent the forces of progress and therefore are justified in taking the measures that 'we' do take. The criticism of 'our' means is thus disarmed by the declaration of 'our' ends, without much recognition that the habitual use of these means is likely to render impossible the realization of the ends. And all through this argument there is a kind of mythologized 'we', a grand appropriation of progress and the proletariat, that constitutes the ultimate hubris of the Bolshevik outlook. (In the twentieth century, the demythologizing of this 'we' has been one of the first steps towards political lucidity.)

None of the immediate issues provoked by the dispute with Kautsky would, in the long run, prove as important as this central premise of Trotsky's book: the identification of the Bolshevik party with the destiny and interests of the working class. A representative passage:

> The continuous 'independence' of the trade union movement, in the period of proletarian revolution, is just as much an impossibility as the policy of coalition [with other parties]. The trade unions become the most important economic organs of the proletariat in power. Thereby they fall under the leadership of the Communist Party. Not only questions of principle in the trade union movement, but serious conflicts of organization within it, are decided by the Central Committee of our party.

In 1936, writing about the Stalin constitution, Trotsky would declare the identification of state and party, party and proletariat, to be 'the fundamental sophism of the official doctrine'. Admittedly there is a large difference between Lenin's Russia of 1920 and Stalin's Russia of 1936. Nevertheless, does not the sophism that Trotsky rightly attacked find at least partial anticipation in the above passage from his own book? To his credit, he does anticipate the counter-argument:

> But where is your guarantee, certain wise men ask us, that it is just your party that expresses the interests of historical development? Destroying or driving underground the other parties, you have thereby prevented their political competition with you, and consequently you have deprived yourself of the possibility of testing your line of action.

Trotsky then offers his answer:

> In a period in which all antagonisms assume an open character . . . the ruling party has sufficient material standard by which to test its line of action, without the possible circulation of Menshevik papers. Noske [the German Social Democrat hated for his role in the death of Rosa Luxemburg and Karl Liebknecht] crushes the Communists, but they grow. We have suppressed the Mensheviks and SRs – and they have disappeared.

Would not the earlier, or the later, Trotsky have found this line of argument embarrassing? For who can believe that 'growth' is necessarily evidence of political correctness? Is not Trotsky's argument all too close to that of his opponents who were to sneer at the pitifully small movement he headed in the 1930s?[1] As it happens, the Mensheviks *did* grow in the early 1920s, at least until they were destroyed by the Cheka. No; this book does Trotsky small honour. If there is a single text that supports those who believe Leninism and Stalinism to be closely linked or to form a line of continuous descent, it is *Terrorism and Communism*.

To pummel Kautsky was easy enough; to cope with the problems described by Kautsky was more difficult. For Trotsky, as indeed for the Bolsheviks as a whole, the moment after victory in the civil war was a peculiarly agonizing one. Nothing had turned out as they hoped, nothing as they expected. They were masters of ruin, lords of hunger. In Europe there had been revolts, uprisings, abortive *coups*, but the rescue of the Russian Revolution by the international proletariat had not come. Large segments, perhaps a majority, of the European working class still clung to the Social Democrats. Among themselves the Bolsheviks knew perfectly well that they retained power in Russia mostly through the army and the police. They knew the Russian peasantry hated the agrarian policies of the regime.[2] They knew the Russian working class had lost most of its revolutionary élan. Power, Lord Acton said, corrupts and absolute power absolutely; but for many kinds of authoritarian elites, especially those not in the grip of ideology, this does not prove very troublesome. Rulers who feel no need to justify their tyranny by invoking high ideals of fraternity and egalitarianism can be quite comfortable with the oppressions they exact, the blood they spill. But for men who have taken power out of a passionate commitment to a great ideal and have never hesitated to sacrifice themselves (and others) on its behalf, it must be profoundly troubling to find that they have ended up as a harsh dictatorial clique, even as they still invoke the slogan of 'the dictatorship of the proletariat'. For some, that sense of trouble may lead to sustained intellectual reconsiderations, for others a sinking into the sloth of bureaucratic cynicism, and for still others a determination to try once again a forced march upon history in the hope of somehow reaching the ideals of earlier years. I am not saying that Trotsky, or the other leading Bolsheviks, consciously took one or the other of these paths. It was too early for that. There was still a great deal of revolutionary will, infatuation with power, insistence upon the ultimate rightness of the ideology of the vanguard. But signs of dismay and doubt start to appear, naturally more visible in retrospect than at the time.

Trotsky oscillated between extreme positions. At one point he anticipated the 'retreat' or relaxation of the New Economic Policy; at another point he drove towards an extensive military communism in the hope of thereby patching together the torn economic fabric of Russia. Other Bolsheviks responded differently. One dissident group within the party – the Workers' Opposition, made up mainly of revolutionary workers and headed by the veteran party leader Shlyapnikov – denounced the entire hierarchic, bureaucratic and military direction which the regime had taken; it demanded that trade unions and workers committees take over the running of the economy. This semi-syndicalist notion clearly threatened the party's monopoly of power, and was probably quite impractical with regard to an economy so chaotic and impoverished. For both reasons, Lenin and Trotsky opposed this group. A second opposition – the Democratic Centralists, composed mainly of intellectuals – demanded a restoration of soviet and party democracy. Speaking on behalf of 'civilian soviet culture', the Democratic Centralists recalled the party to the values Lenin had advanced in his 1917 brochure, *State and Revolution*. Trotsky, by contrast, drove his political logic to an absolute, almost inhuman extreme, arguing that it was necessary in this time of desperation to *increase* the power of the ruling institutions.

The issues festering within the party hierarchy broke out in 1920 as a rather strange dispute known as 'the trade union debate'. Not much was at stake immediately or practically, a very great deal ultimately and programmatically. Trotsky argued that the Russian trade unions must be absorbed into the machinery of government. Lenin, while hardly wishing to grant the unions much freedom of action, still had enough realism to favour a limited autonomy for the unions, seeing them as agencies able to exert pressure on the government on behalf of the workers' immediate needs.

At the famous Tenth Party Congress in 1921 Trotsky argued:

> The party is obliged to maintain its dictatorship, regardless of temporary waverings in the spontaneous moods of the masses, regardless of the temporary vacillations even in the working class . . . The dictatorship does not base itself at every given moment on the formal principle of a workers' democracy, although the workers' democracy is, of course, the only method by which the masses can be drawn more and more into political life.

Even the most dialectical of imaginations would be hard put to deny the multitude of dilemmas this astonishingly candid passage reveals. Perhaps the one saving element in this thrashing about of the Bolshevik leaders during the early 1920s was that within the party debate remained open and sharp, so that a range of opinions could still be heard, including some which in better circumstances might have found release through other parties.

In Europe the Bolshevik regime still commanded support among left-wing publics. Portions of the socialist parties had split off to help form the Communist International. There was widespread hope or illusion about 'the Soviet experiment' – that would last another two or three decades – though it is significant, and more so than the Bolshevik leaders knew or acknowledged, that voices of disenchantment began to be heard in liberal and left-wing circles that could hardly be accused of being enemies of the revolution.

In the spring of 1920 Bertrand Russell paid a brief visit to the Soviet Union and later that year published a small book, *The Practice and Theory of Bolshevism*, which is still worth reading. After announcing himself an opponent of capitalism and an admirer of the ultimate goals of Communism, Russell wrote that the Western friends of the Bolsheviks

> think of the dictatorship of the proletariat as merely a new form of representative government, in which only working men and women have votes . . . They think that 'proletariat' means 'proletariat', but 'dictatorship' does not quite mean 'dictatorship'. This is the opposite of the truth. When a Russian Communist speaks of dictatorship he means the word literally, but when he speaks of the proletariat he means the word in a Pickwickian sense. He means the 'class conscious' part of the proletariat, i.e. the Communist Party. He includes people by no means proletarian . . . who have the right opinions, and he excludes such wage-earners as have not the right opinions . . .
>
> The necessity of inculcating Communism produces a hot-house condition, where every breath of fresh air must be excluded . . . The country comes to resemble an immensely magnified Jesuit College . . .

In the early 1920s the lucidity of Russell's sentences was matched only perhaps by some pieces written by Julius Martov, the tragic figure who was trying, with small success, to serve as a peaceful opposition to the Bolsheviks. Later Trotsky called Martov 'the Hamlet of democratic socialism', without remembering apparently that Hamlet had a gift for noticing what was rotten in Denmark. Here in 1921 is Martov, in one of his last articles before he left Russia:

> The Soviet State has not established in any instance electiveness and recall of public officials . . . It has not suppressed the professional police . . . It has not done away with social hierarchy in production. It has not lessened the total subjection of the local community to the power of the State. On the contrary, the Soviet State shows a tendency in the opposite direction. It shows a tendency towards intensified centralism of the State, a tendency towards the utmost possible strengthening of the principles of hierarchy and compulsion. It shows a tendency towards the development of a more specialized apparatus of repression than before . . .
>
> As [the Bolsheviks] see matters now, the road to the non-Statist social order no longer lies in the progressive atrophy of the functions and institutions that have been forged by the bourgeois State, as they said they saw things in 1917 [e.g. Lenin's *State and Revolution* – I.H.]. Now it appears that their way to a social order that would be free from the State lies in the hypertrophy – the excessive development – of these functions and in the resurrection, under an altered aspect, of most State institutions typical of the bourgeois era. These shrewd people continue to repudiate democratic parliamentarism. But they no longer repudiate, at the same time, those instruments of State power *to which parliamentarism is a counterweight within bourgeois society*: bureaucracy, police, a permanent army with commanding cadres that are independent of the soldiers, etc.

An explosion was inevitable: it came in the winter of 1921. Bands of starving peasants-turned-bandit roamed the countryside. Strikes broke out in major cities. A fuel shortage led to the closing of many factories. The transport workers in Petrograd, while performing heavy labour, received only 700 to 1000 calories of food a day. Hungry workers in the cities improvised expeditions to the country-side, hoping to trade a piece of clothing or a household tool for a bit of food – in defiance of the government ban on free trading. Rebellion smouldered throughout the country.

At the Kronstadt naval base the sailors organized them-selves as an autonomous political force, 'repudiating the local Bolshevik leaders. Led by anarchists, left SRs and free-lance radicals, they raised the perspective of 'a Third Revolution' that would return the impaled Soviets to actual power. They demanded free elections to the Soviets, in which all left-wing parties could freely participate. They demanded freedom of speech and press for 'workers, peasants, and for the anarchists and left socialist parties'. They demanded an economic relaxation: the right of peasants to 'do as they please with all the land ... provided they use no hired labour', and the right to individual small-scale manufacture, again with the same proviso. Not always coherent in their politics, but full of a revolutionary democratic passion, the sailors even won the support of about 30 per cent of the local Communist section.

For the Bolsheviks this posed a major threat. At the Tenth Party Congress Lenin admitted that the Kronstadt rebels 'do not want the White Guards, and they do not want our power either' – a statement far more candid than much of the Bolshevik propaganda at the time, which often tried to smear the Kronstadt rebels with a White Guard brush. The government, however, decided not to compro-mise. On 5 March Trotsky demanded unconditional surrender. When his demand was ignored, the Red Army prepared to attack. Kronstadt is seventeen miles from Petro-grad on the Bay of Finland; troops could reach the island as long as the ice of winter remained thick; but once it melted, the rebels would be almost invulnerable. Delegates from the party's Tenth Congress, including the dissidents of the Workers Opposition and the Democratic Centralists, joined the attack. Covered with white sheets, the troops marched in ghost-like procession across the ice. Shells from Kronstadt shattered the ice; soldiers drowned in the freezing bay; the advancing regiments, finally reaching the fortress, overwhelmed the rebels. Casualties on both sides were heavy, the repressions by the victors brutal.

Reviewing a parade of troops on 3 April, Trotsky declared: 'We waited as long as possible for our blinded sailor-comrades to see with their own eyes where the mutiny led. But we were confronted by the danger that the ice would melt,' and therefore the attack had to be launched.

Returning in 1938 to the theme of Kronstadt because left-wing anti-Stalinist writers were criticizing him for his role in suppressing the revolt, Trotsky remained intransigent. The revolt, he argued, had endangered the Bolshevik regime. If it had been allowed to spread, it might have set off a wave of rebellion throughout the country. Besides, the sailors at Kronstadt were no longer the idealistic revolutionists of 1917, many of whom had been killed in the civil war, but were younger peasant replacements with little political experience. By 1938, however, Trotsky was saying nothing about White Guard leadership or influence.

Even if Trotsky's later arguments are granted, the Kronstadt rebellion marks one of the darkest episodes in the history of early Bolshevism. Fixed into an increasingly authoritarian posture, the regime had no recourse but to use its military might against the discontented and rebellious masses – no recourse as long as it rejected the option of even partial democratization. That the Bolsheviks acted ruthlessly, no one can doubt. According to Victor Serge, there were also feelings of guilt, shame and sadness among the more serious party leaders. Shortly after the Bolsheviks had seized power, one of their own had predicted that the effort to maintain a minority dictatorship could lead only to 'terror'. And it was to terror that they had come.

An atmosphere of gloom hung over the Tenth Party Congress in March 1921. Major changes were obviously required, lest the country rise up in explosive reaction to the hardships of life under the Bolsheviks. Lenin now introduced the New Economic Policy (NEP), which the delegates accepted with a minimum of debate; this policy largely picked up ideas Trotsky had advanced a year earlier but for which he had not fought with sufficient energy. The NEP signified the partial restoration of the free market: the peasant would now be allowed to sell his surplus, private capitalists to run small-scale manufacture within limits, and foreign capitalists to lease and operate for their profit certain areas of the Soviet economy.

Fearing that the economic improvement likely to follow from this policy – an improvement that, in fact, quickly occurred – would embolden elements within the peasantry and intelligentsia fundamentally hostile to the regime, the Bolsheviks decided to link economic easement with political tightening. At Lenin's insistence the Congress passed a resolution prohibiting the formation within the party of organized groupings based on political platforms. Such groupings had been a prominent feature of Bolshevik life since its very beginning, and constituted a main argument of those who felt that at least in its internal organization the party was democratic. This decision soon provided a strong practical and ideological basis for the further bureaucratization of the party under the leadership of the Stalinists. Still, it is only fair to add that the decision was made as a provisional emergency and also provided for setting up internal party forums and discussion bulletins through which party members could express divergent views. At the Congress Lenin said:

> If fundamental disagreements exist [within the party], we cannot deprive members of the Central Committee of the right to address themselves to the party . . . If, for example, questions like the Brest-Litovsk peace arise? Can we guarantee that such questions will not arise? It cannot be guaranteed. It is possible that it will then be necessary to elect by platform [to the Party Congress]. That is quite clear.

Step by inexorable step, through the fatality of its own historical overreaching, and almost as if in accord with some final unstated axiom of Trotsky's 'theory of the permanent revolution', the Bolshevik dictatorship struggled in the agony of its isolation, its decline, its corruption. Trapped by vanguard exclusivism, overwhelmed by the problems of bringing 'socialism' to a bleeding and shattered country, driven by a relentless ideology to measures it had not dreamt of but which time, blood and cynicism made more palatable each day, Bolshevism kept improvising policies at once more liberal and more authoritarian. It stumbled into the Thermidor of Stalinism – but that term, borrowed from the French Revolution, does not even begin to suggest what lay ahead for both the Bolsheviks and the people of Russia. There was one last desperate spasm, with Lenin for a few months, Trotsky for a few years, in which Bolshevism tried to recover its political and moral poise, tried to regain its earlier socialist bearings. But that was to be too little and too late.

4 The Rise of Stalinism

In the years immediately after the revolution, Lenin was often less doctrinaire, less 'orthodox' than Trotsky. Grand theories, extreme oscillations, rigid positions – these were temptations that Trotsky could not always resist. The more pragmatic Lenin opposed Trotsky's facile identification of the Bolshevik state with the proletariat; he had the good sense – it was a matter of keeping one's eyes open – to describe the regime as a *'deformed* workers' state' in which the workers' organizations must defend not only the state against its enemies but themselves against 'their' state. If still far from a consistent democratic view, this allowed at least for a certain realism and flexibility in Lenin's thinking.

In a speech before the Third Congress of the Communist International (1921), Lenin reiterated the premise common to all the Bolshevik leaders:

> Even prior to the Bolshevik revolution, as well as after it, we thought that the revolution would also occur either immediately or at least very soon in other backward countries and in the more highly developed capitalist countries. *Otherwise we would perish.* [Emphasis added – I.H.]

Now, with the disintegration of the Russian economy and the defeat of the 1919–21 revolutions in Europe,[1] there were already signs that Lenin's prophecy would be realized – but in ways neither Lenin nor Trotsky had foreseen. The Bolshevik party could preserve itself as master of a shattered and beleaguered society within the limits of a shrunken Russia; but in doing so it underwent major transformations in political ideology, social character, moral quality.

To prevent economic collapse or social explosion, Lenin proposed as part of his New Economic Policy (NEP) large-scale concessions to an already hostile peasantry; but this in turn helped to bring into existence a whole new stratum of conservative 'rich' and middle peasants.[2] When the mass of soldiers, demobilized after the civil war, came back drained of their revolutionary or patriotic fervour, these conservative tendencies within the countryside were further strengthened.

So too in the cities. The workers were sapped of their social energy. Some had fallen into demoralization, others turned entirely against the regime. Many of the most devoted Bolsheviks had died in the civil war – a fact Trotsky kept stressing as one explanation for the decline in the party's moral level. Others had been worn out, and still others soon came to display the characteristics of bureaucratic officials everywhere, with vested interests of their own that set them increasingly apart from the workers in whose name they ruled. Apart from large amounts of economic help – hardly to be expected at a time of international economic crisis and certainly not encouraged by the repeated Bolshevik declamations of world revolutionary perspective – what the country needed was the ventilation of ideas, a wind of freedom bringing new life and energy. But after 1921 the Bolsheviks refused to allow any party but their own to function legally and thereby contributed to their own degeneration. Each repressive measure undertaken by the dictatorship, even when truly the consequence of an emergency created by civil war or economic collapse, further undermined the moral and ideological claims to which many of its supporters were genuinely devoted. A cancerous social growth flourished within the regime: flourished upon deprivation, cynicism and brutality.

A new social stratum – *it had sprung up the very morning of the revolution* – began to consolidate itself: the party-state bureaucracy which found its support in the technical intelligentsia, the factory managers, the military officials, and above all, the party functionaries, some of them only yesterday proletarians. Narrow in outlook, provincial and boorish in tone, primitive in culture, this new social stratum was marked by a nationalist (sometimes, a Great Russian chauvinist) psychology and an instinctive authoritarianism of approach. It looked upon the workers as material to be shaped, upon intellectuals as propagandists to be used, upon the international Communist movement as an auxiliary to be employed, and upon Marxism as a crude system by means of which to rationalize its ambitions.

To speak of a party-state bureaucracy in a country where industry has been nationalized means to speak of a new ruling elite, perhaps a new ruling class, which parasitically fastened itself upon every institution of Russian life. That many members of this new party-state were unaware of the significance of this process seems clear; it was a historical novelty for which little provision had been made in the Marxist scheme of things, except perhaps in some occasional passages to be found in Marx's writings about the distinctive social character of Oriental despotism. Among some Bolshevik leaders, one gathers from the memoirs of Victor Serge, there were hesitant discussions, troubled conversations indicating that they had come to recognize how sadly flawed their victory had turned out to be. In the corridors, party comrades could indulge in an occasional fleeting murmur about the Leviathan they had created. And Lenin, in the final years of his life, launched a series of attacks on the growth of bureaucratism, keenly perceiving its manifestations if not its causes, and apparently preparing himself for a factional struggle against the new concentration of *apparatchiks* that had Stalin as its leader and spokesman. Though by now desperately ill, Lenin spoke out several times against the growing rudeness within the ruling circles of the party, which he rightly saw as symptomatic of far more serious disorders. In a famous article, 'Better Less But Better', he seemed to be moving towards the idea of creating a semi-autonomous institution that might check the aggrandizements of the party machine – and according to Moshe Lewin's valuable study of the period, there is even a scribbled notation regarding a possible legalization of the Mensheviks, also presumably towards the end of checking bureaucratism. But these were the last desperate thrashings of a leader who had lost control of the historical process he had initiated; and we shall never know whether, or how, the slide into Stalinist despotism might have been halted if Lenin had been able to function politically for a few years longer. In 1928 the Bolshevik leader Nikolai Bukharin, after having joined Stalin to defeat Trotsky and then himself having been shattered by the Stalin machine, remarked that 'the root of the evil is that party and state are so completely merged'. Yes, and there were people languishing in 'the dustbin of history' who had been saying as much for some time.

At precisely which point the revolutionary dictatorship of Lenin gave way to the totalitarianism of Stalin is hard to say. Perhaps profitless too. It was a gradual transformation or, in Marxist terms, a counter-revolution that began during or very soon after the revolution itself, in the inner dynamic of the Lenin regime; came to a decisive moment in the mid-1920s; and reached full expression in the 1930s, with the mass deportation of the peasants, the destruction of the Old Bolsheviks, and the Moscow trials. Having consolidated its power, the new bureaucratic class proceeded to exploit the opportunities for centralized economic planning that are peculiar to a nationalized economy. It undertook a 'primitive accumulation of capital' so cruel as to make the earlier accumulations of bourgeois society seem models of humaneness; and what Marx, whose pages of denunciation of bourgeois accumulation are so ferocious, would have made of the Stalinist experience we can hardly imagine.[3]

Of this whole process Trotsky was a powerful intellectual critic but a not very skilful political opponent. For reasons that none of his biographers or colleagues has satisfactorily explained, he pursued in 1923 and for a time afterward an erratic course, occasionally lashing out in fury against the bureaucratic deformations he witnessed everywhere, sometimes offering through Marxist categories a sharp analysis of this phenomenon, and then succumbing to intervals of silence, illness, and depressed withdrawal.[4] We have reliable accounts of Trotsky dutifully attending a session of the Bolshevik Central Committee, and becoming so absorbed in reading a French novel that he did not even hear the buzz of discussion – which, in his judgement, was by now not worth attending to. What a picture that makes: the former head of the Red Army engrossed in a French novel because he cannot bear to hear the speeches of his comrades!

It was as if Trotsky sensed that the very argument he and Lenin had advanced in the first flush of revolutionary enthusiasm – the Western working class comes to our rescue, 'otherwise we would perish' – now suggested that the rise and victory of Stalinism was inevitable. It was as if he grew heart-sick at seeing what had been happening among the Bolshevik victors: the organized harassment to which Trotskyist leaders, distinguished Old Bolsheviks, were subjected by hooligans in the employ of the party apparatus, the severe threats made against all dissidents within the party, the primitive level of argumentation coming from the Stalinist centre, even the first glimmers of its chauvinism and anti-Semitism. It was as if he felt helpless before a monster he had himself helped to nourish, so that he would lapse into phases of paralysis after a high pitch of historical activism.

But in truth we do not really know, or know enough, about the reasons for Trotsky's crushing defeat in the party. He had never been very skilful at intra-party manœuvring: he was too impatient, too rationalistic, too proud.[5] He had always done better as a freelance Marxist publicist or as a leader of insurgent masses. A good many of the best minds within the Bolshevik leadership – Preobrazhensky, Rakovsky, Radek, V. Smirnov – joined his Left Opposition, but in the struggle for control of the party machine, Trotsky and his allies were hopelessly outclassed. Hopelessly outclassed, perhaps, because control of the party machine *did* mean control of the country!

One might suppose that the struggle for survival in the Communist leadership would have occupied Trotsky's entire energies, but it did not. Indeed, he felt a strong disgust at having to cope with the vulgarities and, after a time, the hooligans of the party machine. To write on topics not directly related to the party struggle seemed refreshing, cleansing. And the idea of a many-sided intellectual life, a universality of mind, obviously delighted him.

In 1922 Trotsky published a curious little book of essays called *Problems of Everyday Life.* We have here an unfamiliar Trotsky, one who brings together a strand of Russian high-mindedness, perhaps even echoes of Tolstoy and Turgenev, with an attentiveness to commonplace existence such as few of the classical Marxists ever displayed. Trotsky the preacher, Trotsky the schoolmaster. Trotsky the moralist: how odd, how priggish, how (at times) charming!

He thunders against the bad habit of drinking vodka – in Russia, a good deal more than mere habit. He tells his comrades, many of them as ill-mannered as the Tsarist officials of yesterday, that civility is quite as much a prerequisite for socialism as are electrification and industrialism. 'Foul language', he sermonizes, 'is a legacy of slavery, degradation, and disrespect for human dignity . . . Our Russian foul language is especially so . . . In our lower classes swearing comes from despair, embitterment and above all slavery, without hope or escape. But the swearing of the upper classes, through the throats of the gentry . . . was the expression of class rule, slave-owners' arrogance . . . The Revolution, despite all its occasional cruelty and the bloodstained mercilessness of its methods, is primarily the awakening of humanity . . .'

(Imagine a gathering of *apparatchiks*, tough old-time party hacks like Stalin, Molotov and Ordzhonikidze, over a good ration of vodka, in their now-comfortable offices, as they amuse one another with jokes about this interloper, this Jew-Puritan, Trotsky, who writes sermons . . . against swearing. God damn, it breaks them up!)

The sensibility that led Trotsky to deplore the habit of swearing and, more important, to write some especially warm passages about the rights of women – 'The revolution would be no revolution if . . . it did not help women, doubly and triply enslaved, on to the path of personal and social development' – this sensibility also prompted him to take up his pen against the tendencies towards philistinism steadily growing among the triumphant Bolsheviks. Russian backwardness had left its stamp not merely upon the old society but also upon its new rulers; the taste of power was heady; the growing isolation of the ruling Bolshevik caste led to coarse justifications of the measures taken to keep power; and for the semi- and ill-educated cadres of the party it was irresistibly tempting to see Marxism as an imperial theology providing all answers and, still more, silencing all questions. It was a golden moment for hacks and boors, home-brewed 'theoreticians' and puffed-up officials to talk nonsense – nonsense backed up by bayonets.

As an educated intellectual Trotsky spoke out against such presumption, even as, in the orthodoxy of his Marxism, he also provided it with a certain unintended support. (Lenin was not nearly so interested in cultural matters, taking an attitude of bemused tolerance towards all forms of literature and art as long as the party's political domination was not threatened – though his own tastes were decidedly traditional.) Nor was Trotsky himself free from the Marxist presumption that would make 'dialectics' a key to all knowledge, or worse yet, its nagging monitor. At one point in the early 1920s he lectured a group of Russian scientists regarding the help they might gain from dialectical materialism. What the scientists felt about this lecture we do not know, though anyone acquainted with scientists can probably guess. But on the whole, within the limits imposed by Leninist Russia, Trotsky stood for cultural openness. Witness his qualified defence of Freudianism against the vulgar-Marxists:

An attempt to declare psychoanalysis 'incompatible' with Marxism and merely turn one's back on Freudianism is too simple, or rather, simple-minded . . . Freudianism is a working hypothesis that can and indubitably does give rise to conclusions and surmises pointing towards a materialist psychology. In due time experimentation will put it to the test.

It was, however, in his writings about literature that Trotsky displayed his full intellectual virtuosity. Had he devoted himself systematically (or better yet, unsystematically) to literature, he might have become one of the great critics of our century. As it is, many of the pieces he wrote on literary themes are still fresh, still vivid with sharp insights and brilliant sentences. In one of his last critical essays Trotsky wrote that the French novelist Celine 'walked into great literature as other men walk into their own houses'. The same could be said about Trotsky himself. He shows the mark of the true critic, which is not system, erudition or opinion, but the gift for evoking a writer's essential quality, his voice, inflection, accent, vision. Here are a few sentences from a 1908 essay on Tolstoy:

> From the landlord's manor there runs a short and narrow path straight to the hut of the peasant. Tolstoy, the poet, was accustomed to walk this path often and lovingly even before Tolstoy the moralist turned it into a road of salvation. Even after the abolition of serfdom, he continues to regard the peasant as 'his' – an inalienable part of his material and spiritual inventory. From behind Tolstoy's unquestionable 'physical love for the genuine toiling people' about which he himself tells us, there looks down upon us just as unquestionably his collective aristocratic ancestor – only illumined by an artist's genius . . .
>
> He never puts his heroes on display, as does Turgenev . . . amid bursts of firecrackers and the glare of magnesium flares. He does not seek out situations for them that would set them off to advantage; he hides nothing, suppresses nothing. He shows us his restless seeker of truth, Pierre Bezukhov, turned at the end into a smug head of a family and a happy landlord. Natasha Rostov, so touching in her semi-childlike sensitiveness, he turns, with godlike mercilessness, into a shallow breeding female, soiled diapers in hand. But from behind this seemingly indifferent attentiveness to individual parts there rises a mighty apotheosis of the whole, where everything breathes the spirit of inner necessity and harmony. It might be correct to say that this creative effort is permeated with an *aesthetic pantheism* for which there exists neither beauty nor ugliness, neither the great nor the small, because it sees the whole of life in the perpetual circuit of its manifestations as great and

beautiful. This is the aesthetic of the tiller of the land, mercilessly conservative by nature. And it is this that lends to the epics of Tolstoy kinship with the Pentateuch and the Iliad . . .

Trotsky's major venture into literary criticism, *Literature and Revolution*, was composed during his summer vacations of 1922 and 1923, an extraordinary feat of concentration when one remembers the pressures under which he was working at the time. Not quite unified yet more than a mere gathering of essays, the book is marked by enormous verbal energy, a brilliance of phrasing that shines through even a somewhat erratic English translation. Away from the harshness of life under War Communism and free, if only for the moment, from the ugliness of Bolshevik factionalism, Trotsky seems to breathe a sigh of relief at once again entering that 'world more attractive' he had always taken the arts to be.

The book divides into two parts: at the outset and in the concluding chapters a theoretical assault on the doctrines of Proletkult, which was then proclaiming the rise of a 'proletarian literature' in the Soviet Union, and a series of chapters, often as acute as they are rash, on contemporary Russian writers, from Biely to Mayakovsky.

Within the self-imposed bounds of Marxism, the theoretical chapters may be regarded as definitive. Trotsky begins with a strong appreciation of the role of tradition, as it refers both to the slow, complex meshings of cultural experience and to the internal dynamics of literary history. It is an appreciation of tradition as keen in its way as T. S. Eliot's but not, of course, derived from so intimate a participation in the actual life of literature.

Though Marx himself took for granted the power of tradition in his scattered remarks on cultural subjects, few Marxists have ever troubled to articulate this view with the care that Trotsky devoted to it. He understands that the tempo of cultural change, necessarily slow and at least partly determined by the inner life of culture itself, cannot be yoked to the tempo of political revolution.

The dramatic upheavals of political life must sooner or later affect the inner character of the arts but cannot drive them, cannot dictate to them, cannot issue edicts and demands. History shows that the formation of a new culture which centres around a ruling class demands considerable time and reaches completion only at the period preceding the political decadence of that class.

That Trotsky fails here to specify what he means by 'considerable time' is not nearly so important as his tacit warning against the assumption that a culture can be called into existence by fiat. Equally notable is the last part of the sentence which links cultural upsurge with political decadence, an idea crucial to the serious study of modernism though not, unfortunately, elaborated by Trotsky.

At this point in his argument, the Marxist schema comes to appear excessively comprehensive and optimistic. So long as a 'proletarian dictatorship' is necessary, there is little possibility that a distinctive proletarian culture can be created – there simply cannot be enough leisure, surplus, comfort, tradition. But once the conditions of material life improve significantly and socio-political tensions lessen to the point where the 'proletarian state' begins to wither away, then 'conditions for cultural creation will become more favourable, the proletariat will be more and more dissolved into a socialist community and will free itself from its class characteristics and thus cease to be a proletariat'. If there is an element of troublesome utopianism in this vision of the future, there is also an insistence upon a powerful Marxist idea largely ignored during the dark age of Stalinism: that the historical mission of the proletariat is self-dissolution. Here Trotsky speaks cogently:

The proletariat was, and remains, a non-possessing class. This alone restricted it very much from acquiring those elements of bourgeois culture which have entered into the inventory of mankind for ever . . . The bourgeoisie came into power fully armed with the culture of its time. The proletariat, on the other hand, comes into power fully armed only with the acute need of mastering culture.

Meanwhile, continues Trotsky, the transition to socialism is bound to entail difficulties of a kind inimical to culture in general and any effort to improvise a 'proletarian culture' in particular. Since this transition must be seen as an experimental phase of man's history in which the lowly and the oppressed struggle towards self-determination, the culture of the transitional era should be largely free of party dictate. 'The domain of art is not one in which the Party is called upon to command.' If Trotsky was prepared to accept only conditionally the view that culture is an autonomous realm of human activity – he insisted that ultimately it remains dependent on 'a material base' and that the party must retain the right to intervene against open political attacks – he sided, during the 1920s, with those Bolshevik intellectuals who took a relatively tolerant view of literary divergences.

But there is another side to Trotsky's book, a side that derives from both ideology and temperament. He can say, admirably enough, that 'a work of art should, in the first place, be judged by its own law, that is, the law of art'. But he then adds, 'Marxism alone can explain why and how a given tendency in art has originated in a given period of history . . .' This ideological arrogance, unbacked by evidence or argument, calls to mind endless and still more dubious claims that 'Marxism alone' can shed light on this or explain that – though the shedding and the explaining do not often follow. A more personal source of Trotsky's historical arrogance is his infatuation with the spirit of dynamism, a fury of change. He keeps criticizing, though usually in a friendly spirit, writer after writer, work after work for lacking the 'dynamic' tension, the urban thrust and drive that seem to him characteristic of a revolutionary era. It is as if he were in search of some quintessential poem or novel that will seize the spirit of the time – some new, shiny, functional work bearing within itself all the strengths of tradition yet rising into the glory of the future.

A touching hope but a vain one and, as it turned out, dangerous too. For such a demand could easily lead to impatience, impatience to intolerance, intolerance to prescription, and prescription to prison. Not that, in relation at least to literature, Trotsky slid down this scale of response. But one can't help noticing a clash between the cool good sense of his literary theory and the fiery ultimatism of his literary temperament. The 'poem of the revolution' cannot be written, at least in the form that Trotsky seemed to want it. Precisely for the reasons he himself doubts the possibility of a 'proletarian culture', so must that poem be marked, pocked, and graced by the bearings of the past. It grows uneasy before the high abstractions of the future, it lives most easily with the puzzlements and quiddities of the present. No wonder the poet Mayakovsky, in an untranslatable pun, joked that even the most cultivated of commissars remains a commissar.

Trotsky's hunger for a poem or fiction that would utterly embrace and reveal the spirit of the time – a hunger not exactly known among twentieth-century revolutionists of both deed and word – leads him at the end of his book into a utopian rhapsody about the spirit of a time not yet visible, the era of Communist man when 'all the vital elements of contemporary art [will be developed] to the highest point'. In that blissful classless future 'man will become immeasurably stronger, wiser and subtler . . . The average human type will rise to the heights of an Aristotle, a Goethe or a Marx. And above this ridge new peaks will rise.'

Several decades ago this passage would be lovingly cited by Trotsky's admirers as evidence of sublimity of vision. Now, in a somewhat cooler time, one may wonder about the relationship between this unqualified utopianism and the kind of politics, harsh with the authoritarian certitudes of Bolshevism in power, that Trotsky had been conducting since the revolution. Nor is it quite certain that a time in which 'the average human type' will rise to the level of an Aristotle or Goethe would strike many of us as a prospect either attractive or even bearable.

The strength of *Literature and Revolution*, apart from its devastation of the notion of 'proletarian literature', lies in the chapters on individual writers – quick, jagged, sardonic, affectionate, admiring, impatient. In writing about the enormously talented Mayakovsky, Trotsky succeeds partly in slipping, so to say, under the poet's skin; he grasps imaginatively the poet's struggle to bring into some workable relation the clamour of self and the turbulence of the world; he notes the poet's weakness for large and grandiose phrases and, Marxist bias aside, celebrates instead the personal and non-political lyrics. By certain readings Trotsky may well be wrong in his estimate of Mayakovsky's work, but that hardly matters when set against the penetration and sympathy of his criticism.

Trotsky is a master of the crisp summary, the synoptic evocation, of a writer's essential voice or spirit. Here he writes about the peasant poet Kliuev:

> He promises paradise through the Revolution, but this paradise is only an exaggerated and embellished peasant kingdom, a wheat and honey paradise: a singing bird on the carved wing of the house and a sun shining in jasper and diamonds. Not without hesitation does Kliuev admit into his peasant paradise the radio and magnetism and electricity; and here it appears that electricity is a giant bull out of a peasant epic and that between his horns is a laden table.

A remark on the work of Andrey Biely:

> It is absolutely irrefutable that the human word expresses not only meaning but has a sound value, and that without this attitude to the word there would be no mastery in poetry or in prose. We are not going to deny Biely the merits attributed to him in this field. However, the most weighty and high-sounding word cannot give more than is put into it. Biely seeks in the word, just as the Pythagoreans in numbers, a second, special and hidden meaning. And that is why he finds himself so often in a blind alley of words. If you cross your middle finger over your index finger and touch an object, you will feel two objects, and if you repeat this experiment it will make you feel queer; instead of the correct use of your sense of touch, you are abusing it to deceive yourself. Biely's artistic methods give

exactly this impression. They are invariably falsely complex.

An evocation of the novelist Boris Pilnyak:

> Pilnyak is a realist and an excellent observer with fresh eyes and a good ear. People and things are not old and worn out for him and always the same, and only thrown into temporary disorder by the Revolution. He takes them in their freshness and uniqueness, that is, alive and not dead, and he seeks support for his artistic order in the disorder of the Revolution . . .
> He takes the Revolution in its periphery, in its back yards, in the village, and mainly in the provincial towns. His Revolution is a small town one. Still, even such an approach can be vital . . . But to be that you cannot stop at the periphery. You have to find the axis of the Revolution which is neither in the village nor in the district. You can approach the Revolution through the small town, but you cannot have a small town vision on it.

Rarely in the Marxist literature, and not often in any other, can one find such lucid and sparkling evocations of a writer's distinctive 'signature'. Finally Trotsky does not quite get to the essential business of literary criticism, the analysis and valuation of texts; what he does might be called pre-criticism, the evocation and placing of writers. It hardly matters. The Marxism he employs, supple and responsive, has been absorbed into the critic's vision, informing rather than imposing itself on the subjects he deals with.

These writings on cultural themes were for Trotsky a kind of intellectual vacation, a pleasant relief from the struggle for power within the Bolshevik leadership which broke out in 1922. Until the late 1920s, criticism of the increasingly oppressive nature of the Bolshevik regime could still be voiced, though only from within its ranks and in the later years, not with impunity. (By the late 1920s the leading Trotskyists were scattered in distant Siberian and Asian exile, quite in the way the Tsar had scattered them a few decades earlier.) One respected Bolshevik oppositionist, a fearless man named Myasnikov, wrote: 'The Soviet power must maintain at its own expense a body of detractors as once did the Roman Emperors.' These simple words, carrying a good share of political wisdom, went unheeded; their author even suffered rebuke from the party's Central Committee. In 1923 Trotsky published a group of articles called *The New Course*, in which for the first time he attempted seriously to explore the social sources and character of Bolshevik bureaucratism.[6] Today, more than a half century later, this work may seem rather mild, even timid, although it contains in embryo almost all the critical themes Trotsky was later to develop in his assault on Stalinism; but one must remember that he was committed to – and by now, alas, had hardly any choice but – a strategy of remaining within the party. Too blunt a criticism, he feared, might provoke extreme counter-measures.

The New Course remains, nonetheless, an important historical document. The main stress is on the relationship between bureaucratism and democracy, as if Trotsky had grasped intuitively what he could not yet state boldly, that here was the central thrust of his criticism. For now, in retrospect, it seems clear that the significance of all the opposition groups within the Bolshevik party, both Trotskyist and non-Trotskyist, was primarily as a series of ill-related efforts to stop or slow the trend towards totalitarianism.

From 1923 onward Trotsky was both political leader and intellectual guide of the Left Opposition in Russia. Painfully aware that he was caught in a moment of social retreat which must prove inhospitable to his austere demands and standards, he fought with intermittent energy, yet always with intellectual flair and personal pride. But he fought on the terrain of the enemy, accepting the damaging assumption of a Bolshevik monopoly of power. As Trotsky saw it, the party was now divided into three main tendencies: his own Left Opposition, a small minority representing the historical idea and tradition of the Bolshevik revolution; the Stalinist centre, essentially a bureaucratic crystallization reflecting the decline of revolutionary élan and the backwardness of Russian society; and the right wing led by Bukharin which, in its wish to make large concessions to the prosperous and middle peasants, verged on 'conciliationism' with the capitalist economic tendencies that had arisen in Russia during the NEP. Trotsky was convinced that politically and intellectually the Stalinist 'centre' had no independent basis of its own and that, sooner or later, it would yield to the more principled, if dangerous, positions of the Bukharinist right. The main conflict of programme lay, in his judgement, between the revolutionary Left Opposition and the 'conciliationist' right. As we can now see, this was a historic miscalculation, a great error – but a great error linked with, and perhaps provoked by, his pioneering analysis of the rising Stalinist bureaucracy.

The very aspects of post-revolutionary Russia which Trotsky saw as conducive to Stalinism – social weariness, endless poverty, lack of culture, asphyxiation of independent thought, loss of spirit among the Bolshevik cadres – all this made it almost inevitable that Trotsky, even if he had been tactically cannier than he actually was, would fail. Years earlier, in 1909, he had provided a vivid anticipation of such circumstances:

> When the curve of historical development rises, public thinking becomes more penetrating, braver and more ingenious . . . But when the political curve indicates a drop, public thinking succumbs to stupidity. The priceless gift of political generalization vanishes somewhere without leaving a trace. Stupidity grows in insolence and, baring its teeth, heaps insulting mockery on every attempt at a serious generalization. Feeling that it is in command of the field, it begins to resort to its own means.

Many centuries earlier Thucydides had offered a classical description:

> Those who enjoyed the greatest advantages were the men of limited intelligence. The consciousness of their inability and of the talent of their adversaries made them fear that

they would be duped by the fine speeches or the subtlety of spirit of their enemies and therefore they advanced straight towards their aim; while the others, scorning even to foresee the schemes of their adversaries and believing that action was superfluous when talk seemed to suffice, found themselves disarmed and defeated.

In a bitter turn of events Trotsky was suffering from the vindication of his own theory, by means of which he had foreseen that in a backward country the proletarian revolution would, if it continued to suffer isolation, find itself in a historical dead-end – though how terrible that would be he had not been able to predict. The more subtle the writings of Trotsky and his collaborators were – and many of their writings, especially those by Trotsky, Preobrazhensky and Rakovsky, remain impressive – the more they seemed to undermine their political position. Ascribing the rise of Stalinist bureaucratism not to mere personal factors but to deep-rooted social phenomena, Trotsky and his friends lost in political assurance as they gained in intellectual clarity. Wrote Rakovsky:

By means of demoralizing methods, which convert thinking communists into machines, destroying will, character and human dignity, the ruling [Stalinist] circles have succeeded in converting themselves into an unremovable and inviolate oligarchy, which replaces the class and the party.

To illuminate what was happening in Russia during the mid-1920s, Trotsky brought to bear upon a new, indeed, unprecedented situation categories drawn from a familiar segment of the past. Up to a point, this was an appropriate thing to do: it is a necessity of systematic thought, though it always carries the danger of failing to acknowledge historical novelty. Trotsky borrowed the term 'Thermidor' from French revolutionary history – Thermidor (July) being the month in 1794 when Robespierre was overthrown by the conservative wing of the Jacobins. The 'Thermidorean reaction' brought to an end the radical period of the French Revolution yet did not signify a liquidation of its 'basic social conquests', that is, the destruction of the monarchy and the enablement of bourgeois economy. According to Trotsky, a similar process had now begun in the Soviet Union : the political heirs of October had been defeated but the socio-economic foundations of the workers' state remained. Some years later Trotsky summarized 'the social meaning of the Soviet Thermidor' :

> The poverty and cultural backwardness of the masses has again become incarnate in the malignant figure of the ruler with a giant club in his hand. The . . . bureaucracy, from being a servant of society, has again become its lord. On this road it has attained such a degree of social and moral alienation from the popular masses, that it cannot now permit any control over either its activities or its income.

In his remaining years Trotsky continued to pursue this historical analogy, even to the point of indicating where, with Stalin's increasingly personal dictatorship, there had occurred a turn from Soviet Thermidor to Soviet Bonapartism. It is a fascinating instance of the fusion, or confusion, of scholasticism and intellectual penetration. Among the Russian Trotskyists there were abstruse discussions on whether Thermidor had finally triumphed in the Soviet Union; and it will come as no surprise to those familiar with the habits of Marxist thought that these discussions, probably extending to no more than a few hundred people, should have aroused strong responses among the opposing Bolshevik groups. The Bukharinists and even some of the Stalinists were privately sensitive to the possibility that what Bukharin called the Left Opposition's 'unforgivable chatter about Thermidor' touched on an unwelcome truth. The more sophisticated among them understood that what Trotsky was invoking was not, or not yet, the spectre of a personal dictatorship such as would in fact arise soon enough. He was invoking something that, to them, seemed more terrifying and real : an unbraked social process, a decline of revolutionary energy following upon weariness, error and incapacity. What reason was there to suppose that the Bolsheviks, for all their pride of doctrine, would be able to resist the fate that had overtaken previous revolutions, the fate of disillusion and degeneration, a bloody denial of the ideals for which pure-spirited men had shed their blood?

Tactically it was probably a blunder for Trotsky to employ these historical analogies, since they succeeded mainly in irritating waverers and enraging opponents, some of whom did not exactly have the French Revolution at their fingertips. Intellectually, the frequent return to Thermidor and Bonapartism suggested the extent to which Trotsky was struggling with the darkest of forebodings, the dreaded thought that all had ended in a great debacle.

In one respect the constant harping on the French Revolution proved to be a barrier to political understanding. It tended to blur the uniqueness of the Russian revolutionary experience, it tended to underestimate the crucial ways in which 1917 was different from 1789. Especially (if we may fall back for a moment on Marxist categories) did it pass over the crucial point that a bourgeois revolution can, for a time at least, proceed successfully without the direct political rule of the bourgeoisie, while a proletarian revolution, since undertaken by a class always propertyless, can fulfil its aims only if it keeps the control of the state. Thermidor cut down the radical wing of the French bourgeoisie, but did not threaten bourgeois property; Stalinism cut down the radical wing of the Russian proletariat (as Trotsky saw it), and left the proletariat defenceless before the assaults of the state. Or put in 'ordinary' language: bourgeois economy can survive under a democracy, an old-fashioned dictator, a fascist regime, but socialism can be built, if at all, only as a free and conscious human process, as the popular outgrowth of democracy. It was this crucial point that the Thermidorean analogy blurred – indeed, the failure to grasp it was partly responsible for the capitulation of a good many Trotskyists, once Stalin undertook his super-industrialization and forced collectivization in the late 1920s.

In any case, if it was true that Soviet society was experiencing a time of reaction – a *new kind* of reaction peculiar to the decline of a 'workers' state' – then the theoreticians of the Left Opposition, as serious Marxists, could hardly expect that mere intellectual clarity (the most brilliant of theses) or political fortitude (their hardened revolutionary courage) could change things in any fundamental way. Through only one path might Trotsky have wrested power, and that was a military coup, taking advantage of his popularity in the Red Army. Was this a real possibility or just a fantasy indulged by Western observers? We cannot know for certain. What we do know is that Trotsky never considered it a serious option. For a military coup would have hastened the very authoritarian decline he was fighting against, merely changing the name of 'the Soviet Bonaparte' from Stalin to Trotsky. Trotsky was too much the man of ideological rigour, too much the self-conscious historical actor living by a vision of honour, to sink into the smallness of such an adventure. Those who faulted him for not taking such a course failed to understand either the man or his ideas.

The programmes advanced by Trotsky and his collaborators during the 1920s are far too complex and deeply embedded in the circumstances of the time to allow for quick or easy summary. Still, a few major themes can be noted.

As an orthodox Marxist, Trotsky began with the economic crisis in which Russia found itself. Through a graphic phrase, soon to be picked up by economists throughout the world, he described the problem as that of 'the scissors', the two blades of which, moving farther and farther apart from one another, were the rising prices of industrial goods and the declining prices of agricultural goods. The peasants could not afford to buy industrial goods and had little incentive for selling their produce. If widened much farther, the 'scissors' would break, thereby endangering the fragile alliance between city and country, worker and peasant.

Trotsky, together with his brilliant economist colleague Preobrazhensky, argued that in the long run the problem could be solved only through a lowering of industrial prices, so as to enable the peasantry to engage in a fuller economic exchange with the city and to increase its productivity through co-operatives and the necessary process of mechanization. But this, admittedly, was a long-run perspective, and to realize it a comprehensive plan for the revival, modernization and growth of industry was first required. The Left Opposition put forward an elaborate plan aimed at strengthening the 'socialist' industrial sector, raising the productivity of labour, improving the living standards of the workers and drawing them into a more active role in economic life, and supporting the poor peasants against the kulaks (wealthier peasants). The Opposition proposed that wages of workers be raised in order to achieve a rise in performance and productivity; that workers be free to bargain with industrial administrations; that indirect taxes, falling most heavily on the poor, be lowered and the 'NEP bourgeoisie' be taxed more heavily; that the lowest level of the peasantry be exempt from taxation and a progressive tax placed on the remaining peasants, with the heaviest burden falling on the kulaks; and that steps be taken to persuade the peasants, gradually and of their own free will, to enter collectivization.

On a theoretical level, the most ambitious economic scheme associated with the Left Opposition was advanced by Preobrazhensky (not always with the complete agreement of Trotsky, who felt that his collaborator was too rigid, too inclined to see economic decisions apart from political contexts). Russia, said Preobrazhensky, still had to go through the trauma of 'primitive socialist accumulation', that process of capital accumulation which he saw as parallel to, yet qualitatively different from, the 'primitive capitalist accumulation' Marx had described so vividly in *Capital*. Because of the prevailing low levels of productivity, the obsolescence of much industrial plant, and the relatively narrow industrial base in what was still largely a peasant economy, it could not be expected that the nationalized industries would themselves yield sufficient savings to enable this 'primitive socialist accumulation' to proceed with sufficient rapidity. Nor could there be much hope for capital inflows from abroad. In the initial and most difficult phase of accumulation, large quantities of capital could be drawn mostly 'from sources lying outside the complex of state economy' – which meant, for the most part, from the wealthier kulaks who had been doing well under the NEP. Preobrazhensky, as a serious thinker, used the Marxist term "exploitation' to describe the proposed relationship between state and kulaks, though he emphasized that on principle he rejected violence or confiscation as methods of dealing with the peasants. What he favoured was a political-economic tilt, the state to pursue 'a price consciously aimed at the exploitation of the private economy', or what he called a 'non-equivalent exchange' between industry and the countryside.

The major theoretical antagonist of Preobrazhensky and, of course, Trotsky was Bukharin. While also accepting industrialization as a prerequisite for that economic plenty which all Marxists took to be essential for socialist development, Bukharin argued that the Trotskyist proposals would put 'such intense pressure on the peasantry' as to produce a situation 'economically irrational and politically impermissible'. He feared the Trotskyist policy would lead to a breaking of the 'scissors', with the peasantry growing rebellious and refusing to yield its grain except under the kind of duress that had made the years of War Communism so bloody and exhausting. 'Socialist industrialization', he wrote, 'is not a parasite process in relation to the countryside . . . but the means of its greatest transformation and uplifting.' Holding to a kind of Bolshevik neo-populism, Bukharin argued for a slower tempo of industrial development, a pricing policy that would be more accommodating to the peasants, and in effect a mixed economy flowing out of the NEP. Thereby, class antagonisms would be softened rather than sharpened and the Russian people allowed a respite of peace and conciliation.

Bukharin admitted that his proposed policy meant that socialist construction would proceed 'at a snail's pace', and in criticism of this view Trotsky replied that unless there were a rapid expansion of industrial resources it would be impossible to satisfy the demands of the Russian peasantry and 'a gradual back-sliding into a *muzhik* [peasant] thermidor' would result. It seems, in retrospect, that these formidable antagonists were grappling with the opposite terms of an enormous socio-economic dilemma and that each saw clearly the weaknesses in the proposals and arguments of the other.

Meanwhile, though for a time siding with Bukharin, Stalin was a great deal more concerned with gathering the reins of power into his hands than with judging the niceties of theoretical disputation. Though involving urgent and major decisions of policy, these debates concerned matters inherently so difficult and were couched in a Marxist vocabulary so proudly recondite, that they could rarely be grasped by the rank-and-file members of the Bolshevik party, let alone ordinary Russian workers. It was relatively easy for the Stalinist machine to exploit the growing anti-intellectualism which always accompanies moments of social retreat; it was not hard for Stalin, borrowing and vulgarizing Bukharin's arguments, to accuse the Trotskyists of 'underestimating' and wishing to exploit the peasantry. (Didn't Preobrazhensky himself use the word 'exploitation'? That he meant it in the technical Marxist sense, which is something different from its popular usage, was not a point that many of Stalin's supporters troubled to emphasize.)

It seems clear, from the vantage-point of half a century later, that insofar as we separate these debates from the soiling context of Bolshevik factionalism, they formed an early effort to grapple with the difficult problems faced by all underdeveloped nations – capitalist, socialist, whatever – when they try to pull themselves up to the world of modern economy. Who shall pay the heavy social costs, how much one generation can or should be made to sacrifice itself on behalf of an untested future, whether turning for help to developed nations involves too high a political price – these questions, common to our time, were largely anticipated in the Bolshevik discussions of the 1920s. Trotsky and Preobrazhensky were scornful of the newly concocted theory of 'socialism in one country' which Stalin and Bukharin were toying with; the Left Opposition was correct in its insistence that this theory ran against the fundamental premises of Leninism; nevertheless, the painful reality of their situation forced them, in effect, to consider economic options that had as their tacit premise the possibility that the Soviet Union would not be 'rescued' by the world revolution. Somehow, they had to confront the unpleasant problem of what Marxists in power would do if, instead of beginning with a base of industrial plenty, they had first to create it. Could that be done without violating basic socialist premises? Martov and other Mensheviks had warned that it probably could not. A 'socialism of poverty', they had argued, would only lead to new modes of exploitation, new modes of autocracy. And now, like it or not, the Bolsheviks were facing precisely the dilemmas they had contemptuously dismissed as Menshevik phantasms. At the Twelfth Party Congress in 1923 there occurred a highly significant confrontation which Deutscher reports in his biography of Trotsky:

In the debate Krasin, Trotsky's old comrade, addressed himself directly to Trotsky and asked whether he had thought out to the end the implications of primitive socialist accumulation? Early capitalism, Krasin pointed out, did not merely underpay workers or rely on the entrepreneur's 'abstinence' to propose accumulation. It exploited colonies; it 'pillaged entire continents'; it destroyed the yeomanry of England; it ruined the cottage weavers of India and on their bones . . . rose the modern textile industry. Did Trotsky carry the analogy to its logical conclusion?

Krasin put the question without hostile intent. He approached it from his particular angle: as Commissar of Foreign Trade he had tried to persuade the Central Committee of the need for more foreign trade – and of the need to make more concessions to foreign capital. He wished to impress on the congress that since as Bolsheviks they could not expropriate peasants and plunder colonies – everyone took this for granted – they must seek to attract foreign loans; and that foreign capital might help Russia to proceed with primitive accumulation and to avoid the horrors that had accompanied such accumulation in the West. The Bolsheviks, however, had found out by now that they had little chance of attracting foreign credits on acceptable terms; and so the question which Krasin posed retained its full force: where would the resources needed for rapid accumulation come from? When Krasin spoke of the plunder of the peasantry and the 'white bones' of the Hindu cottage weavers, Trotsky jumped to his feet to protest that he had 'proposed nothing of the sort'.

True, Trotsky had proposed nothing of the sort. But Krasin's question, which had its link to Bukharin's arguments, suggested a serious difficulty in Trotsky's position. Granted the validity of Trotsky's claim that a democratization of Soviet economic life might lead to growth in both production and productivity ('Soviet democracy has become an *economic* necessity,' he wrote); granted that the economic proposals of the Left Opposition would improve the functioning of the economy without fatally disrupting the ties between city and countryside. Granted all this and more, what should or could be the economic perspectives of the regime if, despite the best strategic guidance from Moscow, the revolution in the West was not forthcoming and help therefore not available? To this question Trotsky could hardly reply by merely repeating with Lenin that unless the revolution did triumph in the West 'we would perish'. It was one thing to advance this as a general theoretical proposition for an entire historic era; it was quite another to make it the basis of policy for a government ruling over millions of people. Trotsky's position, charged his opponents, left no visible avenue of retreat, no fall-back in case it turned out that the Bolshevik regime would for a time have to go it alone. And indeed, if one were to follow the usual Trotskyist accounts, as well as Deutscher's biography, it would be hard simply to dismiss this criticism.

But a recent specialized study by Professor Richard Day of Trotsky's economic policies makes it clear that, in addition to his proposals for industrialization in the Soviet Union and a reinvigorated Leninist revolutionary policy throughout the world, Trotsky did try to confront the immediate economic difficulties of Russia in realistic terms. He felt, apparently, that Preobrazhensky's scheme for 'non-equivalent exchange' between countryside and city would not suffice for providing the necessary 'primary socialist accumulation' and/or that it might be open to the difficulties (peasant rebellion, etc.) upon which Bukharin kept harping. He understood also that from within its own resources Soviet industry could not provide a large enough surplus for the rate of industrialization he envisaged. Consequently, in his economic proposals he did turn to the West – the capitalist West which, he thought, might for reasons of its own be willing to advance the stabilized Russian regime the capital it urgently needed. And for this, he was prepared to consider offering 'concessions' to private Western interests, quite as Lenin had been willing a few years earlier, though without much success. I quote now from Professor Day :

In 1920–1 Trotsky had believed that Russia was too poor to attract foreign capital on a sizeable scale. Since that time recovery had been completed. A more pronounced imperialist struggle would also be accompanied by vigorous competition to secure and monopolize raw materials. With America intruding upon established European sources of supply it seemed reasonable to suppose that Russia might now provide a plausible alternative. Speaking to a delegation of German workers in July 1925, Trotsky argued: 'We ourselves have been extremely cautious, one might even say too cautious with respect to concessions agreements. We were too poor and too weak. Our industry and our entire economy were too ruined and we were afraid that the introduction of foreign capital would undermine the still-weak foundations of socialist industry . . . We are still very backward in a technical sense. We are interested in using every possible means to accelerate our technical progress. Concessions are one way to do this. Despite our economic consolidation, or more precisely, because of our economic consolidation, we are now more inclined than a few years ago to pay foreign capitalists significant sums for . . . their participation in the development of our productive forces . . . We are in need of credit, and we need concessions as well in order to speed up our economic growth and thereby to increase the well-being of the masses.'

Somewhat later, in preparation for a party congress, Trotsky elaborated these views into a theoretical statement:

Actually, the most essential line of our economic growth is precisely the fact that we are at last leaving behind our closed state-economic existence and are entering into increasingly profound ties with the European and world markets. To reduce the whole question of our development to the internal relation between the proletariat and peasantry in the USSR [a thrust at Bukharin – I.H.], and to think that correct political manoeuvring . . . frees us from world economic dependencies, means falling into a dreadful national limitation.

And again, sharply put:

We must renew our basic capital, which is presently passing through a crisis. Whoever imagines that we will be able to build all of our equipment in the coming years, or even the greater part of it, is a dreamer. The industrialization of our country . . . means . . . not a decrease, but on the contrary, a growth of our connections with the outside world . . . which means . . . our growing dependence . . . on the world market, on capitalism, on its technical equipment and its economy.

Or, as Professor Day summarizes this position, 'By developing foreign trade with the West, Russia would both anticipate and prepare for the world revolution . . . Russia's reunification with Europe was to begin far in advance of the revolution in the West; Russia would 'grow' into Europe, and this economic symbiosis would later find political expression in an international socialist federation.'

As Trotsky was thus forging this elaborate synthesis of bold revolutionary and uncertain practical schemes, he was attacked by Stalin and Bukharin not only as a 'super-industrializer' but for turning excessively towards the West. On Stalin's part, some of this was mere factional demagogy, appealing to the encrusted dogmatism of party stalwarts; some of it, perhaps, anticipated his later policy, which would press towards industrialization by leaving behind both 'capitalist' and 'socialist' methods and norms. Bukharin's opposition to Trotsky's scheme for cautious economic relations with Western Europe is harder to understand, since one might suppose that his idea of 'a snail's pace' within Russia would go well with credits from and concessions to Western capitalist interests; perhaps it was that Bukharin was now Stalin's political ally and simply had to go along with the current line.

One may suggest, then, that even as Trotsky hewed to his basic revolutionary perspective, he understood that meanwhile, until the happy advent of the 'European socialist federation', measures were needed to cope with Russian economic difficulties and that foreign credits might soften the predictable hardships of development. This, in a sense, was an equivalent – different in specific proposals but similar in purposes – to Bukharin's programme. Both accepted a continuation of the NEP but differed as to which segment of the economy should be given the greater aid; both advanced programmes far less extreme and ruthless, and much closer to the animating political-moral norms of traditional socialism, than would Stalin after his consolidation of power.

In these circumstances, we may now wonder, was there not a kernel of wisdom in Bukharin's vision of a sort of Bolshevik-dominated mixed economy – assuming one could detach it from his indefensible political alliance with Stalin? Might this not have been a way of accommodating the increasingly isolated and unpopular regime to the vast peasant masses and thereby avert or minimize repression? Would not a moderate economic development together with at least a partial democratization, and perhaps accompanied by some economic concessions to European capitalism in return for credits and a partial accommodation with the European Social Democracy, have been a course that might have spared twentieth-century Russia at least some of its agonies? Such a course might have required the Bolsheviks to acknowledge that, far from building 'socialism in one country', they were embarked on a policy recognizing the social and economic absurdity of that notion – they were undertaking, preliminary to socialism, a gradual modernization under the control of the state but with concessions to the market. More important still, such a course would have meant acknowledging that the very conception of socialism with which they had begun had shown itself to be rigid and unworkable, and that it required modification towards what would later come to be called 'market socialism'.

Whether such a course could have succeeded in view of the enormous internal social difficulties in the Soviet Union, the atmosphere of political repression, and the hostilities encountered from capitalist powers abroad, we cannot know. The difficulties that Trotsky and his associates emphasized in arguing against such a possibility were real enough. But in retrospect it is at least arguable that, despite the major differences between Trotsky and Bukharin, both were in fact advocating versions of Bolshevik 'moderation' in economic policy. Had Trotsky prevailed, it would probably not have been possible to maintain so stringent a 'primary socialist accumulation' as Preobrazhensky envisioned, for it would have been necessary to take into account the wishes and resistance of the peasantry. Had Bukharin prevailed, it would probably not have been possible to yield as much to the peasants as he advocated, since that might have threatened the stability of Bolshevik rule. What actually happened was something far more stringent, fearsome, and 'radical' than either Trotsky or Bukharin dreamt of. The totalitarian Stalin regime left behind the norms and limits of both 'capitalist primary accumulation' and 'socialist primary accumulation'; it transformed the state into a merciless agent of exploitation, in both the 'scientific' Marxist and popular senses; it undertook a *civil war by the state against society*, creating thereby a kind of Oriental-industrial tyranny which dragged a portion – not more than a portion – of the Russian economy into the modern era while pulling Russia backward socially, towards a despotism unequalled by the cruellest of the Tsars.

Some years later, when Stalinism had completely

triumphed and a good number of Western liberals had succumbed to an uncritical acceptance of its claims, it became fashionable to say that Stalin, having embarked on a frenzied programme of industrialization, had 'stolen Trotsky's thunder'.[7] This sort of argument, often no more than a cynical sneer, ignored a point which Trotsky insisted was crucial: that what mattered was not industrialization itself but industrialization on behalf of socialist ends and achieved through socialist means. Industrialization might, after all, be effected in any backward country prepared to employ centralized power with sufficient ruthlessness in order to sweat a large enough surplus out of its population. That, everyone understood. But for Trotsky industrialization mattered as a means for 'raising the specific gravity of the proletariat in society', and thereby moving towards the harmonious realm of socialism. By contrast, Stalin's industrialization was achieved through a social exploitation and political demoralization of the working class unprecedented even in the Industrial Revolution of the West. It was achieved by the destruction of all autonomous political life, or what little remained of it, and the imposition of a totalitarian terror. It brought grave economic imbalances, profound social disruption, extreme political barbarism. It exacted a cost of millions of lives in the countryside and untold horrors in the slave labour camps.

No; this was not the 'thunder' that Trotsky or any other Bolshevik leader of the 1920s had proposed. An observation by one of Trotsky's former collaborators, Max Shachtman, is worth quoting here:

The workers' power in Russia, even in the already attenuated form of a dictatorship of the Bolshevik party, stood as an obstacle in the path of [capital] accumulation precisely because, on the one hand, socialist accumulation was impossible under conditions of an isolated and backward country and, on the other hand, workers' power was incompatible with any other kind of accumulation. This power, then, had to be shattered.

Shattered, that is, by the Stalin dictatorship.

For Trotsky, the proposals made by the Left Opposition for economic planning were inseparable from its demand that party democracy be revived. A later generation, however, may be forgiven if it sees the issue of democracy as crucial and regards Trotsky's sustained critique of Stalinism as his great contribution to modern thought and politics. Begun in 1923 and continued until his death in 1940, this critique touched upon every area of social life: from the bloody horrors of Stalin's forced collectivization to the Byzantine corruptions of the 'personality cult', from the regime's benighted policies regarding such matters as abortion to its brutal attitudes towards cultural life, from its great Russian chauvinism to its sly indulgence in anti-Semitism. Is there another instance in modern history where a powerful mind directed itself with such persistence and passion to exposing the false claims of a regime that still commanded the loyalties of millions of people throughout the world? In the course of this cleansing and heroic assault, Trotsky no doubt made errors, but often enough it has been upon the foundation of these pioneering errors that later analyses have been built. Though contemporary students of totalitarianism may diverge at crucial points from Trotsky, almost all of them owe him a large debt. For it was he who first struggled with the problems of Stalinist totalitarianism, he who suffered ridicule and contempt, not only from befuddled fellow-travellers but also from wilfully enraptured liberals who refused to believe the simple but, for them, unbearable truths about Stalinism.

'Free discussion within the party has in fact disappeared,' wrote Trotsky in the early years of the factional struggle:

> In these times the broad masses of the party do not nominate and elect the provincial committees and the Central Committee . . . On the contrary, the secretarial hierarchy of the party to an ever greater degree selects the membership of conferences and congresses, which to an ever greater degree are becoming executive consultations of the hierarchy.

Now perhaps too late, Trotsky turned back to that vision of participatory socialism which Lenin had advanced in *State and Revolution* and which in the early 1920s had played no particular role in the political life of either Trotsky or his opponents.

We must not build socialism [wrote Trotsky in 1925] by the bureaucratic road, we must not create a socialist society by administrative orders; only by way of the greatest initiative, individual activity, persistence and resilience of the opinion and will of the many-millioned masses, who sense and know that the matter is their own concern . . . only in these conditions . . . is it possible to build socialism.

In proposing a renewed freedom of discussion within the Bolshevik party, Trotsky did not take the next step of proposing a restoration of freedom for the outlawed socialist parties – and for this failure he must be sharply criticized. In 1917, a few weeks before the October revolution, when Trotsky was elected President of the Petrograd Soviet, he had promised: 'We shall conduct the work of the Petrograd Soviet in a spirit of lawfulness and of full freedom for all parties.' Towards the end of his life he wrote:

In the beginning, the party had wished and hoped to preserve freedom of political struggle within the framework of the Soviets. The civil war introduced stern amendments into this calculation. The Opposition parties [Menshevik, SR, etc.] were forbidden one after the other. This measure, obviously in conflict with the spirit of Soviet democracy, the leaders of Bolshevism regarded not as a principle, but as an episodic act of self-defence.

The reality seems to have been more complex than Trotsky here acknowledged and decidedly less flattering to 'the leaders of Bolshevism'. By the mid-1920s, if not earlier, it may not have been a 'principle' of Bolshevism to insist that only one party could function legally, but it was certainly a good deal more than 'an episodic act of self-

defence'. Even in *The New Course*, the work that marks
the emergence of Trotsky as critic of the repressive tendencies embodied in Stalinism, he could still write: 'We are
the only party in the country, and in the period of the
[proletarian] dictatorship, it could not be otherwise.' Bukharin's contribution to this theme was the long-famous and
disastrous joke that in the Soviet Union there could be
numerous parties: one in power, the others in jail. There
was no need for the Bolsheviks to make the one-party
society a 'principle' when, in fact, they were making it a
habitual and unquestioned practice.

All the experience of our century inclines us to suspect
the argument from necessity by which Trotsky, in his later
years, justified the suppression of dissident parties. Even if
one grants some force to his claim that it was a require-
ment of the harsh civil-war years, one must also heed, for
example, the careful and persuasive documentation of
Leonard Schapiro's *The Origin of the Communist Autocracy*, an account of the repeated violations of democratic
procedures by the Bolshevik regime in the years between
1917 and 1922, a good many of which could not possibly
be attributed to the pressures of the civil war. In any case,
Trotsky's decision to limit himself during the factional
struggles of the 1920s to a demand for democracy within
the Bolshevik party placed him in a severe contradiction.
Democracy within a ruling party, especially if it dominates
a society in which property has become the possession of
the state, is finally impossible unless it is extended beyond
the limits of that party. Trotsky was demanding both a
monopoly of power and a monopoly of freedom for the
Bolsheviks: something barely possible for a brief interval,
but surely not for longer.

There is no reason whatever to suppose that if Trotsky
had raised the demand for multi-party democracy it would
have strengthened his cause or re-established his popularity.
By then, and for this Trotsky had to assume a share of
responsibility, articulate or active political publics no
longer existed in the Soviet Union; they had been destroyed
by the Bolshevik regime; and as a result, there was, in one
sense, 'no one' to appeal to out there, beyond the limits

of the ruling party – 'no one', that is, except the wearied and increasingly disillusioned workers, 'no one' except the scattered remnants of the other parties, either fearful of being chewed up in intra-Bolshevik struggles or privately wishing a plague on all their houses, Trotskyist, Stalinist, Bukharinist. A demand for multi-party democracy would have isolated Trotsky still further within the Bolshevik hierarchy, and very likely would by now have sparked no great enthusiasm among the masses. But it would have made his political and moral position more secure in the eyes of that historical posterity upon whose verdict Trotsky seemed to bank so heavily.

Still, one can understand why the idea of multi-party democracy had so little currency, except perhaps among a tiny minority of dissidents who had decided that Trotsky did not go far enough, that the Bolshevik party was hopelessly corrupted and a 'new revolution', the 'third revolution' of which the Kronstadt rebels had spoken, was now needed. By the mid-1920s, the over-all atmosphere in the Soviet Union was so largely drained of revolutionary élan or hopefulness that to the beleaguered group of Old Bolsheviks who gathered about Trotsky the idea of multi-party democracy, if it occurred to them at all, would have seemed utopian, an irrelevance. It was hard enough, often impossible, to gain a hearing within the party, let alone think of going beyond it. To say this is not to excuse the principled failure of Trotsky to raise the issue of multi-party socialist democracy; it is, at best, to explain it.

A pall of apprehension hung over the Bolshevik leaders, those few score of ideologues and party bureaucrats who ruled the nation. What the Opposition said, even some of its opponents secretly feared to be true: that a grey reaction was engulfing the country so completely, it left even the most strong-willed revolutionaries with a sense of bafflement. At the Fourteenth Party Congress in 1925, the last that Trotsky attended, there occurred a remarkable, chilling incident. Zinoviev and Kamenev, yesterday Stalin's allies in the war against Trotskyism, had themselves gone into opposition and were now being stripped of their powers by the Stalin-controlled delegates. Bukharin, still the ideological ally of Stalin though in a short time also to be cut down by him, supported Stalin's measures. As Isaac Deutscher recounts it,

> Kamenev protested. It was strange, he said, that Bukharin, who had always opposed drastic reprisals against the Trotskyists, should now call for the whip. 'Ah, but he has come to relish the whip,' Trotsky interjected. Bukharin, as though caught off guard, cried back: 'You think I have come to relish it, but this relishing makes me shudder from head to foot.'

And not Bukharin alone! Others also shuddered 'from head to foot'. But a process had been unleashed, a demon in part of their own making, which the Bolshevik leaders could not control. For a short while, in 1926–7, the United Opposition (Trotsky together with Zinoviev and Kamenev) tried going to the rank and file of the party, hoping there to find some support. In his memoirs Victor Serge describes one such meeting:

> Smilga, an economist and former army leader who in 1917 had been Lenin's confidential agent in the Baltic fleet . . . spoke for a whole evening in a little room to about fifty workers who could not move at all, so closely were they squeezed together . . . Smilga, sitting on a stool and in the middle of the room, spoke, in an expert's tone and without one agitational phrase, of production, unemployment, grain and budgetary figures, and of the Plan we were hotly advocating. Not since the first days of the Revolution had the Party's leadership been seen in an atmosphere of poverty and simplicity like this . . .

To little avail. When Trotsky and other leaders of the Opposition appeared in Moscow factories to appeal to the rank-and-file workers, the party machine greeted them with organized booing, physical intimidation, and other hooligan methods. Less than a decade after the revolution, its great orator could not make himself heard before an audience of workers. Worst still, as Trotsky saw it, was that the

workers usually stood by passively, not interfering with
the party goons, showing themselves either apathetic or
fearful. This was not the Moscow proletariat of 1917 or
even 1920. It was too late.

So it was to be with every Opposition group, from
Trotsky's in 1923 to Bukharin's four or five years later.
The party machine, with its ubiquitous and menacing
General Secretary, ruled over almost everything, guarantee-
ing itself at party elections majorities of more than 90 per
cent (in some instances, a solid 100 per cent), driving
critics into exile, silencing the handful of remaining independent voices. Later historians of anti-Stalinist radicalism
have often wondered why it was that the Trotskyist and
Bukharinist oppositions, weak as both finally turned out
to be, did not unite or at least form a bloc to defend party
democracy.[8] In part, this was rendered impossible by
mounting factional hatreds; in part, by a shared Marxist
assumption that made each group feel its differences over
economic policy were more important than the question
of democracy. Each underestimated the significance of
Stalin as a historic figure and Stalinism as a historic
phenomenon; each failed to grasp the extent to which the
new power in the Soviet Union would act apart from and
in violation of their shared premises. Trotsky kept describing the Stalinists as 'the centre' of the party, a 'centre'
wavering between the proletarian internationalism of the
left and the neo-populist conservatism of the right.
Bukharin inverted the value terms of this analysis yet
shared the view that the Stalinists represented nothing
very much ideologically. This was true only if one kept
to the traditional bounds of Marxism-Leninism, only if
one kept to the terms of belief and analysis that finally
Trotsky and Bukharin shared. But it was not at all true
if one saw that an entire historical mutation was in process
of birth, something far beyond the intent or grasp of any
of the traditional Bolshevik thinkers.

Trotsky believed that in alliance with the new conservative elements in the countryside, whose interests he saw
reflected in the programme of Bukharin's Right Communists, the party bureaucracy might constitute a nucleus

for the restoration of private capitalism. For some years, in his searching analyses of Stalinism, he would be on the lookout for symptoms of such a 'restoration'. He could not find it, because it was not there. Actually, the new ruling stratum with Stalin at its head, as it gathered into its hands control of the state and society, had every interest in *preventing* a return to private capitalism. It neither owned nor could own property, but instead controlled the state in whose legal custody property resided. Private capitalism would have meant the end of its power and privilege; bureaucratic collectivism was the basis for extending that power and privilege. It would therefore have been entirely appropriate, certainly no violation of principle, for the two main Opposition groups to have made a bloc against the rising bureaucracy, even if there is little reason to suppose that this would have significantly altered the course of events.

By 1929 Stalin had consolidated his power. The Left Opposition was crushed, the Right Opposition rendered helpless. Trotskyist leaders were driven into exile or silence in prison, and Trotsky himself was sent to a distant region of Asian Russia and early in 1929 deported from the country. A pall of obedience fell over Russia, an obedience that in its deepest qualities seemed as old as Russia itself but in its justifying ideology unique to our century. And then came the terror.

5   Wandering, Exile, Work

And now begin Trotsky's years of wandering. No longer
were there masses of cheering listeners to inflame with his
eloquence; no longer armies to spur into heroism, parties
to guide towards power. The most brilliant figure of the
Russian revolution was cast by the usurping dictatorship
as a heretic, then a 'traitor', and finally, in the macabre
frame-ups of the Moscow trials, an 'accomplice of fascism'.
   A harassed and powerless exile, Trotsky continued to
speak and write defiantly. Sharper and wittier than ever,
his pen became his sole weapon, quite as it had been in
1903 or 1912 : a comparison that pleased and consoled him.
In Russia most of his followers had either been broken or
thrust into the far reaches, the freezing wastes, of the
Arctic. Elsewhere, his following consisted of tiny sects of
young people, sincere, largely inexperienced, sometimes
feckless. Personal tragedies, incalculable sufferings beset
him, but he remained erect and combative, faithful to his
vision both in its truth and error, insight and blindness.
Even those rejecting his every word must recognize that
in the last ten or twelve years of his life Trotsky offered
a towering example of what a man can be.
   He was driven from country to country. Each time he
found a place of exile – Turkey, France, Norway, finally
Mexico – the local Stalinists and fascists, as well as the
diplomatic representatives of the Russian regime, whipped
up agitation demanding that he be sent away. His very
presence could still make governments uncomfortable,
summoning images of revolt, fears of the unruly depths.
These governments might succumb to Stalinist pressure but
they knew better than to believe Stalinist propaganda.
They knew Trotsky remained a revolutionist to his bones.
   There is a story, Shakespearian in quality, that may
stand as emblematic of Trotsky's experience during these
harsh years. In 1936, when he was living as an exile in

Norway, its Social Democratic government placed him under house arrest, precisely at the moment he was being vilified at the Moscow trials as a 'fascist agent'. The Norwegian Minister of Justice, Trygve Lie, a leading Social Democrat and later to be Secretary General of the United Nations, insisted that Trotsky agree not to respond publicly to the trials and also to submit his correspondence to censorship – an outrageous demand that would in effect have forced Trotsky to political suicide and that probably was made as a result of pressures from the Soviet Union.

His voice rising with scorn, Trotsky replied to Lie:

This is your first act of surrender to Nazism in your own country. You will pay for this. You think yourself secure and free to deal with a political exile as you please. But the day is near – remember this! – the day is near when the Nazis will drive you from your country, all of you . . .

Lie shrugged. He held power, Trotsky did not. Let Isaac Deutscher continue the story:

Yet after less than four years the same government had indeed to flee from Norway before the Nazi invasion; and as the ministers and their aged King Haakon stood on the coast, huddled together and waiting anxiously for a boat that was to take them to England, they recalled with awe Trotsky's words as a prophet's curse come true.

Through all these years Trotsky lived in constant danger of assassination. Each of his residences had to be turned into an armed camp. He chafed under these restrictions, for he liked freedom of movement and took pleasure, as a physically vital man, in fishing off the Turkish coast or gathering cactus in Mexico. He must also have known that against the resources of the Russian secret police (the GPU), there could hardly be an adequate physical defence. In Mexico, before Trotsky was finally murdered in 1940, the talented Communist painter David Siqueiros organized a terrorist raid on his house. In Europe a number of

Trotsky's political associates were murdered by agents of the GPU.

The vengeance of the Kremlin was directed not merely against Trotsky himself, or his phalanx of active followers, but also against the members of his family, whether or not they were politically active. His first wife, Alexandra Sokolovskaya, remained an unrepentant Oppositionist and even though an elderly woman by now, was banished to distant exile and apparently died there. The two children Trotsky had with her also came to tragic ends. In Moscow both were severely harassed by the regime and their husbands, Oppositionist stalwarts, shipped off to exile. One daughter, Nina, died of illness while Trotsky was in Turkey. The other daughter, Zinaida, a brilliant high-strung woman, spent some time with her father in Turkey, but there were clashes of temperament, and soon it became clear that she was in a perilous psychological state. Zinaida went to Berlin, where she lived for a time in near-destitution, and then, in 1933, committed suicide. This brought from her mother in Leningrad an anguished letter to Trotsky: 'I explained to [Zinaida] that all this comes from your character, from the fact that you find it so difficult to show your feelings when you would like to show them.' She added: 'Our children were doomed.'

The younger son by Trotsky's second marriage, Sergei, was a scientist who on principle had kept away from politics, though remaining personally loyal to his father. In 1937 he was arrested and charged – nothing was too preposterous those days – with planning 'a mass poisoning of workers'. Sent to the Vorkuta labour camp in the distant Arctic, Sergei, though still refusing to label himself politically, joined the Trotskyists there in a hunger strike; and then, brought back to Moscow, he held out steadfastly against all the GPU's attempts to have him repudiate his father. In the late 1930s this admirable young man was shot.

The other son by Trotsky's second marriage, Leon Sedov, followed closely in his father's political footsteps, serving as a spokesman in Europe, publishing the Russian-language *Bulletin of the Opposition*, bearing the brunt, while over-

worked, penniless and lonely, of his father's constant
demands for greater energy in exposing the Moscow trials
and advancing the political cause they shared. In 1938, at
the age of 32, Sedov died under mysterious circumstances
in a Paris hospital. His friends suspected the GPU. The
stricken father seemed suddenly to age and after locking
himself away for days to mourn with his wife, he turned
again to his pen – there was nothing else – and wrote an
austere threnody : 'He was part of us, our young part . . .
Together with our boy has died everything that still
remained young in us . . . we have not been able to save
you.'

Towering over this doomed family, binding it with ties
of affection, and sometimes serving as mediator between
its overstrained members, stood Trotsky's second wife,
Natalya, a woman of resolute sweetness and goodness, in
the line of the heroines of Turgenev. She had never cared
much for the tokens of power in Russia, having preferred
to occupy herself with cultural matters; now, she bore the
ordeal of exile with a fortitude almost awesome. The
relationship between husband and wife was tender, solici-
tous, deeply respectful. In his 'Diary in Exile' Trotsky
writes at one point that he had been reading the autobiography of Protopop Avakuum, a seventeenth-century
Christian heretic who, with his wife, had suffered persecution, disease, starvation and exile. Adds Trotsky :

> Reflecting on the blows that had fallen to our lot I reminded
> [Natalya] the other day of the life of the Archpriest Ava-
> kuum. They were stumbling on together in Siberia, the
> rebellious priest and his faithful spouse. Their feet sunk in
> the snow, and the poor exhausted woman kept falling in
> the snowdrifts. Avakuum relates : 'And I came up and she,
> poor soul, began to reproach me, saying, "How long, Arch-
> priest, is this suffering to be?" And I said, "Markovna, unto
> our very death." And she, with a sigh, answered : "So be
> it, Petrovich, let us be getting on our way."'

Through all these years there would be no surcease from
the assaults of the Stalin dictatorship and its secret police.

Their *agents provocateurs* wormed their way into Trotsky's movement, the most successful and deadly being Mark Zborowski who under the pseudonym of Etienne enjoyed Trotsky's closest confidence. (Years later this unsavoury figure, his past still hidden, was welcomed into the American academic community as co-author of an 'anthropological' study of the *shtetl* in Eastern Europe.[1]) And from Russia there kept leaking out reports of the humiliations to which once-proud colleagues such as Preobrazhensky, Smilga, Pyatakov and Rakovsky had been reduced. As for the fate of the unbroken Trotskyists who still survived in the Arctic circle – their last desperate hunger strike maintained for 132 days, followed by mass executions – this was not yet fully known during Trotsky's lifetime.

Caustic and proud, shaking off his personal griefs in order to return to the discipline of work, Trotsky continued to write his trenchant analyses of the totalitarian regime in Russia, exposing before a disbelieving world (rather, a world that did not want to believe) the terrorism which Stalin was directing against helpless millions. Time blurs memories, the shame of those years is covered by apologia. It becomes acutely urgent to remember that a good portion of the Western liberal and radical intelligentsia was celebrating the wisdom and humanity of the Stalin dictatorship – some of these people did not acknowledge the truth about the Moscow trials until Khrushchev finally revealed it in 1956, and then only because it was he who revealed it. All through the 1930s Trotsky stood almost alone in pointing to the facts – for they were facts – about the Stalin regime.

Step by step he followed the transformation of the Stalin dictatorship into a full-scale totalitarian state, denouncing the economic policies by which the regime aggravated the exploitation of the masses on behalf of its mania for super-industrialization, enriching (though sometimes also confusing) his description of Stalinism with analogies drawn from the French Revolution, and riddling the claims of those Western liberals who had begun to praise the Soviet Union only after it had sunk into totalitarianism. Again and again Trotsky was accused of exaggeration and spite; the American liberal weeklies printed recondite discussions of the 'psychological causes' behind his attacks; but almost everything he wrote would later be confirmed by the revelations that started coming out of the Soviet Union after Stalin's death. When Trotsky published in 1937 his essay 'Thermidor and Anti-Semitism', in which he accused the Stalinist regime of a surreptitious anti-Semitism, even some of his followers felt a little uneasy: had not 'the Old Man' gone too far? As it turned out, he had hardly gone far enough.

The man who emerges in these concluding ten or twelve years is a figure of greatness, but flawed greatness: a man great in personal courage and intellectual resources, but flawed in self-recognition, in his final inability or refusal to scrutinize his own assumptions with the corrosive intensity he brought to those of his political opponents. He is now an all too human figure. He is often nervous. He is subject to psychosomatic complaints. He alternates between periods of ferocious work and sluggish withdrawal. He feels guilty with regard to his children, all of whose lives, in one way or another, have been sacrificed in the political struggle. He is afraid that he may die before finishing his revolutionary task. He is overcome by the incongruity between the magnitude of his political perspective and the paltriness of his political means. He becomes aware, with a sudden chill, of the rush of time. ('Old age', he notes in his diary, 'is the most unexpected of all the things that happen to a man.') Yet he works with incomparable self-discipline. He abandons, when he deems it necessary, the crowning work of his life, an uncompleted biography of Lenin, to drudge at what he regards as the necessities of polemicizing against dissident comrades, replying to the assaults of Moscow, and writing books to support his household. Unburdened by office he is again the independent political analyst, historian and literary man. He writes now with an authority of statement, an incisiveness of structure, a cutting sharpness of phrase, a flowing range of metaphor that demand that he be regarded as among the great writers of his time. And his productivity is amazing.

Perhaps nowhere else did these talents shine forth so brightly as in Trotsky's writings in the early 1930s on the rise of Nazism. These consist of articles and pamphlets composed hurriedly in exile: there is no effort to work out a theoretical synthesis, partly because Trotsky's major objective is to offer tactical guidance for preventing Hitler's victory and partly because the phenomenon of Nazism is still new. But such brilliant works as 'Germany, the Key to the International Situation' (1931), 'What Next?' (1932), 'The Only Road' (1932) and 'What Is National Socialism?' (1933) contain within them many of the elements needed for a theory of Nazism. Later writers on this subject have given Trotsky credit for insisting that only a united front of the left could stop Hitler, but perhaps because his theoretical insights are scattered – and one must remember they were put to paper before Hitlerism could reveal itself in power – there has not been enough acknowledgement of how keenly he grasped the character of Nazism.

Trotsky placed the rise of Nazism in the context of a mounting crisis of capitalism, not just one of those cyclical or conjunctural disturbances that break out periodically. This breakdown signifies that for capitalism to survive it must abandon the luxury of parliamentary democracy and hand over its political fate to the fascists. Economic benefit will be accompanied by political loss, reinforcement of capitalist property by political retreat of the bourgeoisie. But fascism represents something radically different from traditional police states or dictatorships; it is a mass movement, drawing upon disaffected and rejected portions of the population, and it creates conditions of mass terror – partially before and completely after taking power – that result in the destruction of all working-class organizations and indeed all possible centres of social resistance and political independence. This mass movement draws support primarily from the lower middle class or petty bourgeoisie, driven to desperation by inflation, unemployment, bankruptcy and social instability. 'The petty bourgeoisie, at the very beginning of the crisis, has already assumed a position antagonistic to the *present system* of capitalist rule, but at the same time mortally hostile to the proletarian revolution.' The victory of fascism as a mass movement is predicated on previous failures of the working class to seize the political initiative and thereby resolve the crisis of society.

At least in its broad strokes, this analysis could be acceptable to other students of fascism, both Marxist and non-Marxist. Differences arise when we come to the period after Hitlerism has taken power. Does the big bourgeoisie – say, the Krupps arms trust – still retain decisive socioeconomic influence even though its representatives may have been deprived of direct political power, or does the new regime acquire an 'independent character', as a totalitarian state committed to its own expansionist drive, blending terror and ideology on behalf of a self-determined dynamic of power? Trotsky never succumbed to the vulgar-Marxist notion that Hitlerism was merely 'the naked dictatorship of the bourgeoisie'; but he tended to believe that there would occur, once the Hitlerites came to power, an interpenetration between traditional big bourgeoisie and newly arisen Nazi bureaucracy, with the result not merely a stabilization of capitalist economy but at least a partial reassertion of political authority by the bourgeosie. That capitalist economy survived and thrived under Hitler is beyond doubt; precisely what the relations of power were between the big bourgeoisie and the Nazi elite seems more problematic. In any case, Trotsky did not live long enough to probe the latter question with any thoroughness or to examine it in light of the inner development of Nazi Germany during the Second World War.

I have given the bare schema of Trotsky's approach to fascism, but the richness of his analysis lies in specific descriptions and anticipations. Here he speaks in 1931 about the probability of Nazi terror:

> The coming to power of the National Socialists [Nazis] would mean first of all the extermination of the flower of the German proletariat . . . Considering the far greater maturity and acuteness of the social contradictions in Germany, the hellish work of Italian fascism would probably appear as a pale and almost humane experiment in

comparison with the work of the German National Socialists.

Here he describes, in 1932, the role of the petty bourgeoisie:

> [Fascism] raises to their feet those classes that are immediately above the proletariat and that are ever in dread of being forced down into its ranks; it organizes and militarizes them at the expense of finance capital, under the cover of the official government . . . Fascism is not merely a system of reprisals, of brutal force, and of police terror. Fascism is a particular governmental system based on the uprooting of all elements of proletarian democracy within bourgeoisie society.

Here he turns, in 1933, to the role of *Der Führer*:

> At the start of his political career, Hitler stood out only because of his big temperament, a voice much louder than others, and an intellectual mediocrity much more self-assured. He did not bring into the movement any ready-made programme, if one disregards the insulted soldier's thirst for vengeance . . . There were in the country plenty of ruined and drowning people with scars and fresh bruises. They all wanted to thump with their fists on the table. This Hitler could do better than others. True, he knew not how to cure the evil. But his harangues resounded, now like commands and now like prayers addressed to inexorable fate. Doomed classes, like those fatally ill, never tire of making variations on their plaints nor of listening to consolations. Hitler's speeches were all attuned to this pitch. Sentimental formlessness, absence of disciplined thought, ignorance along with gaudy erudition – all these minuses turned into pluses.

And brilliantly, in 1933, on the general characteristics of fascism:

> Fascism has opened up the depths of society for politics. Today, not only in peasant homes but also in city skyscrapers, there lives alongside of the twentieth century the

tenth or the thirteenth. A hundred million people use electricity and still believe in the magic power of signs and exorcisms. The Pope of Rome broadcasts over the radio about the miraculous transformation of water into wine. Movie stars go to mediums. Aviators who pilot miraculous mechanisms created by man's genius wear amulets on their sweaters. What inexhaustible reserves they possess of darkness, ignorance, and savagery! Despair has raised them to their feet, fascism has given them a banner. Everything that should have been eliminated from the national organism in the form of cultural excrement in the course of the normal development of society has now come gushing out from the throat; capitalist society is puking up the undigested barbarism. Such is the physiology of [Nazism].

But Trotsky's main purpose in these writings was not to provide a full-scale theory of fascism, but to stir the German left towards concerted action. With blazing sarcasm and urgency – he never could be patient towards fools – he attacked the preposterous policy of the German Communists, who in their ultra-left 'third period' were declaring the Social Democrats to be 'social fascists' representing a greater danger than the Nazis.[2] Trotsky kept insisting on what in retrospect seems utterly clear and simple: that only a united front ('march separately, strike together') of the Communists and Social Democrats could stop Hitler. Some of his most trenchant pages are devoted to the 'Red Referendum', the suicidal tactic by which the Communists in Prussia joined the Nazis in 1931 to topple a Social Democratic provincial government. Trotsky writes with a will-to-patience that barely masks a burning impatience: how can the German Communists be so blind? Don't they see that if Hitler takes power, he will destroy *all* the left-wing parties? In an article written in December 1931, 'For a Workers' United Front Against Fascism', he keeps hammering away: there is only a little time left, you can still reinvigorate the ranks of the German working class through united action to stop the Nazi hooligans:

For the feebleminded let us cite another example. When

one of my enemies sets before me small daily portions of
poison and the second, on the other hand, is about to shoot
straight at me, then I will first knock the revolver out of
the hand of my second enemy, for this gives me an opportunity to get rid of my first enemy. But that does not at all
mean that the poison is a 'lesser evil' in comparison with
the revolver.

In a prophetic vein, directly to the militants of the left:

Worker-Communists, you are hundreds of thousands,
millions; you cannot leave for any place; there are not
enough passports for you. Should fascism come to power,
it will ride over your skulls and spines like a tank. Your
salvation lies in merciless struggle. And only a fighting
unity with the Social Democratic workers can bring victory.
Make haste, worker-Communists, you have very little time
left!

And in 1932, after steadily pounding away at these truisms,
Trotsky's impatience bursts through and he appends to
'What Next?' a stinging conclusion 'attributed' to Aesop's
Fables:

A cattle dealer once drove some bulls to the slaughter-
house. And the butcher came nigh with his sharp knife.
'Let us close ranks and jack up this executioner on our
horns,' suggested one of the bulls.
'If you please, in what way is the butcher any worse
than the dealer who drove us hither with his cudgel?'
replied the bulls, who had received their political education
in the institute of Manuilsky [secretary of the Comintern
under Stalin].
'But we shall be able to attend to the dealer as well
afterwards.'
'Nothing doing,' replied the bulls, firm in their principle,
to the counsellor. 'You are trying to shield our enemies
from the left; you are a social-butcher yourself.'
And they refused to close ranks.

Had Trotsky's advice been followed (the Stalinists

attacked him for 'capitulating' to Social Democracy!) the
world might have been spared some of the horrors of our
century; at the very least, the German working class would
have gone down in battle rather than allowing the Nazi
thugs to take power without resistance. But Trotsky was
not heeded. His flow of articles and pamphlets barely
reached the larger left-wing public.

Devastating as was his polemic against the theory of
'social fascism', there yet remains a problem. How, one
must wonder, could the Communist movement, even in
its Stalinist decadence, advance a theory not merely bizarre
but insane in its evident consequences? Say what you
please about the Social Democrats: excoriate them as
traitors, feeble pawns of the bourgeoisie, etc. Still, it seems
almost beyond credence that the German Communists
should have failed to see that it was the Nazis who formed
the greater danger. One plausible but insufficient explanation is that within the Soviet Union there was occurring
the worst phase of the forced collectivization, a kind of
civil war by state against people, and that an ultra-left
international policy was its natural accompaniment. Still,
the German Communists were staking their heads on this
theory of 'social fascism' – how could they?

There is no easy answer, once we acknowledge that all
theories of politics tend to underestimate the role of
human stupidity. Nevertheless, it may be worth speculating
about the notion – I advance it gingerly – that in an
extremely distorted way the theory of 'social fascism' had
a subterranean link with a part of Bolshevism that Trotsky
preferred not to consider. The Bolshevik preoccupation
with the unique historical mission of 'the vanguard party'
(that is, the Bolsheviks themselves); the Bolshevik insistence
that competing parties within the socialist spectrum were
not merely wrong but necessarily reflected alien class
interests; the Bolshevik commitment to 'clearing the
ground' of rival left-wing groups – all of these elements of
monolithic politics may have found a parodic extension in
the theory of 'social fascism'.

That Lenin would have regarded the theory of 'social
fascism' as pernicious nonsense, and that many of the

Bolshevik leaders now captive to Stalin's terror must privately have regarded it in the same way – of course! Yet it was a kind of nonsense they had perhaps helped to spawn, the detritus of their authoritarian pride. The theory of 'social fascism' in relation to Bolshevik vanguardism: was that not, just a little, like Smerdyakov in relation to Ivan Karamazov?

The failure of both the Social Democracy and the Communists to resist Hitler's assumption of power, seemed to Trotsky an event of enormous importance. It signified the utter bankruptcy of both traditional reformism and Stalinism, together commanding over twelve million votes in German, to show any fighting spirit, not for the revolution but for sheer survival. He concluded that on an international scale it was now time to start afresh, with a mere handful, in order to create a new Marxist – the Fourth – International. This ill-starred venture absorbed most of his political energies during his remaining years, and now, in commenting on the political turmoil of France and Spain during the mid-1930s, he wrote no longer as an Oppositionist critic within or near the Communist movement but as leader of a new political movement, trying to nurture it into revolutionary strength.

In brochures like 'Whither France?' and a whole series of articles on Spain, Trotsky displayed both the analytic powers and ideological rigidities of his Marxism. The pieces on Spain probed the difficulties, familiar enough to a Russian Marxist, of modernizing a stagnant country. They stressed, on the one hand, the indigenous militancy of the Spanish working class (which had a strong anarchist tradition) and, on the other, the backwardness of the Spanish bourgeoisie which, like its pre-October Russian cousin, would block measures towards reform or even a dynamic economy because of its social cowardice and greed. Thereby, the country must be thrown into a major social crisis for which the ruling powers would see a 'solution' only in fascism. About the Spanish Civil War itself there is no comprehensive work by Trotsky, only a running series of short pieces, letters and interviews. What has happened in Spain, he writes, is not merely a fascist counter-revolution; there is also occurring simultaneously the beginnings of a social revolution within the Loyalist camp: peasant expropriations of land and worker take-overs of factories, especially in Catalonia. For the military struggle against Franco to be successful, it is necessary to push this working-class action to fulfilment, thereby satisfying the demands and arousing the enthusiasm of the masses and, at the same time, undermining Franco's political support. Some of the elite troops in the fascist army were Moors and if, urged Trotsky, a demand were popularized for the freedom of Spanish Morocco – something which the republic until then had been unwilling to do – then it might be possible to stimulate mass defections. Clearly, while trying to respond to what was distinctive in the Spanish situation, Trotsky still had in mind the model of October. In 1937, for example, he writes:

In Spain the Stalinists, who led the chorus from on high, have advanced the formula to which Caballero [the Socialist], president of the cabinet, also adheres: first, military victory, and then social reform. I consider this formula fatal for the Spanish revolution. Not seeing the radical differences between the two programmes in reality [of the fascist and republican sides], the toiling masses, above all, the peasants, fall into indifference. In these conditions, fascism will inevitably win, because the purely military advantage is on its side. Audacious social reforms represent the strongest weapon in the civil war and the fundamental condition for the victory over fascism.

Somewhat later, in response to questions at the Mexico City hearings on the Moscow trials, Trotsky elaborated the same views:

The only possible way to assure victory in Spain is to say to the peasants: 'The Spanish soil is your soil.' To say to the workers: 'The Spanish factories are your factories.' . . . It is necessary to fight. But, you know, it is not sufficient to fight with a gun. It is necessary to have ideas and give these same ideas to others, to prepare for the future. I can fight with the simple peasant, but he understands very little in the situation. I must give him an explanation. I must say : 'You are right in fighting Franco. We must exterminate the fascists, but not in order to have the same Spain as before the civil war, because Franco issued from this Spain. We must exterminate the foundation of Franco, the social foundation of Franco, which is the social system of capitalism.'

During the social upheavals that convulsed Europe in the 1930s, Trotsky turned to France. He analysed the Popular Front that had been formed by the Socialists, Communists and the Radical Socialists (a liberal bourgeois party) as an inherently unstable amalgam that lacked coherent purpose or will. He made a sharp distinction between a united front, which involves limited agreements among working-class parties confined to specific immediate needs (e.g., common defence against fascist attack) while leaving each party free to advance its own political ideas, and a popular front, which brought together working-class and bourgeois parties in an unacceptable union that necessarily blocked revolutionary possibilities. Excessively hopeful, Trotsky saw the French working class as striving towards revolutionary action – there were large-scale strikes – but restrained by corrupted leaders.

Neither about Spain nor France does Trotsky's analysis now seem quite persuasive. That bourgeois democratic society in Western Europe found itself in such difficulties as to raise doubts about its capacity to survive; that there were urgent criticisms to be made of both the Social Democrats and Stalinists; that the workers of France and Spain were, in varying degrees, restive – all this was true. Spain, indeed, had some of the elements that Marxists have seen as part of a 'revolutionary situation' : more so in radical Catalonia than elsewhere. But there were also strong reasons for calling into question Trotsky's apparent scenario of a Spanish October. The Soviet Union, now in alliance with the Western democracies, played a very strong role in shaping the politics of the Spanish republic, both inhibiting tendencies towards radical transformation and provoking a repressive campaign against dissident leftists; the fascist troops, powerfully aided by Hitler and Mussolini, were close at hand and far from experiencing the kind of defeat and demoralization that had made the Russian army vulnerable to radical propaganda in 1917; the general political atmosphere of Europe was now far worse, with the fascist powers in the ascendancy and both the democracies and the left-wing movements in retreat; and within Spain itself, despite the strength in Catalonia of the POUM, an anti-Stalinist leftist but not Trotskyist party, the mass of the workers still remained loyal to their traditional organizations : Socialist, anarchist and, in lesser degree, Communist. The Russia in which the Bolsheviks had taken power was a disorganized country, with vast social and geographical spaces, and this proved to be a large advantage to the Bolsheviks, allowing them room for manœuvre and retreat; the Spain of the late 1930s was politically and socially 'crowded', with little entry-space for a revolutionary insurgency.

Many of these factors Trotsky himself acknowledged, but argued that if only there were a revolutionary party in Spain all might yet be transformed. But precisely this 'subjective' factor must, in its very magnitude, also be seen as part of the 'objective' situation. Why could there not develop in the West European countries significant revolutionary parties? Was it merely due to the inexperience and ineptitude of their leaders? Was it merely that the Stalinists, with the resources of Moscow behind them, remained so powerful? Or was it that the very idea of *a historical repetition* in the form Trotsky proposed had lost its powers of attraction, its inspiring mystique? The failure to construct a new revolutionary movement may, after all, have had something to do with the fact that, while loyal to the traditional radical parties and prepared to fight defensive actions against fascism, the working class of Western Europe was simply not inclined to take the Leninist path. Had it really ever been? Perhaps it was too weary after decades of struggle and division; perhaps it had been shaken by the terrible events of Russia in the past decade; perhaps it retained a stronger attachment to parliamentary democracy and its own autonomous organizations than Trotsky was prepared to acknowledge; perhaps even the Western Communists sensed, in some corner of their consciousness, that the path of the Russian Bolsheviks could not be their path. It is impossible to measure these things with any accuracy, for we are speaking about social moods and political possibilities. Had the Socialists and Communists in Spain declared a Soviet republic, or something like it, one suspects that the majority of the Spanish workers would have been ready to go along with them; but clearly they were not ready to break from the Socialists and Communists in order to declare a Soviet republic. Trotsky counted too heavily on revolutionary will, revolutionary clarity, revolutionary élan; he could not allow himself to see the extent to which 1937 was sharply different from 1917 and Western Europe sharply different from Russia.

All the while, Trotsky kept working to create a new movement of the revolutionary left, the Fourth International, which would be loyal to the original principles of Marxism-Leninism. This effort failed – failed, as we can now see, dismally. The masses of radical workers in Europe showed no interest in the tiny Trotskyist or other sects, while those intellectuals who broke away from Stalinism often found themselves reconsidering and then abandoning the whole Leninist outlook. From a Marxist point of view, the 1930s were a time of retreat, not advance, a time of bewilderment and demoralization under the blows of fascism and Stalinism. This was hardly the atmosphere in which a new revolutionary vanguard could be created. Except for a few veteran leaders who had left their Communist parties, like Alfred Rosmer in France and Henricus Sneevliet in Holland, the Trotskyist cadres in Europe were green, untested and quite unable to meet the pressures to which they were subjected by enemy movements and governments. The more independent and experienced Marxists who had at first associated themselves with Trotsky – men like Rosmer and Sneevliet, also Andres Nin in Spain and Victor Serge in France – soon broke with him politically, often feeling, despite their respect and admiration, that he remained too rigid in his loyalty to the Bolshevik tradition.

In 1936, impatient with the weakness of his international following, Trotsky proposed the temporary dissolution of the independent Trotskyist groups and the entry of their members into the socialist or Social Democratic parties. It cannot be said that this manœuvre was undertaken in good faith. What might have become a reconciliation of the scattered forces of the anti-Stalinist left soon ended as a raid by the reassembled Trotskyists upon the socialist parties. In two or three years the Trotskyists were expelled, emerging as slightly larger sects, but only after having earned the enmity of a good many left-wing socialists who intellectually were not very far from them. In the United States this manœuvre, boasted the Trotskyist leader James P. Cannon, had effectively destroyed what remained of the Socialist party, and for once he was right. Only in two distant outposts of civilization, Ceylon and Bolivia, did the Trotskyist groups take on the character of a popular movement – an oddity that made clear, by contrast, how completely it failed in the major industrial countries to attract even a solid core of 'advanced' left-wing militants.

As a political leader in these years Trotsky tended to be fractious and inflexible: he had never been very adept as the head of small groups. In what almost seemed an eagerness to alienate precisely those who were coming closer to his views, he composed numerous polemics against the 'centrists', that is, the left-wing socialists who had broken away from the mass Social Democratic parties but were not yet prepared to accept the full catalogue of Trotskyist doctrine. Especially revealing is a running exchange of letters between Trotsky and Andres Nin, leader of the Spanish POUM, who had succeeded in building, as no one else in Europe had, a left-wing anti-Stalinist party considerably larger than the hermetic Trotskyist sects. Between the two men there was a bond of mutual respect, yet Trotsky could not keep himself from trying to shape Nin's political course according to the Bolshevik idea while Nin, struggling to maintain his party in a desperate situation, felt that he had to work out his own, indigenous Spanish strategies.

By another reckoning one can find a measure of pathos in the effort of the revolutionary exile to pass on the word to the novices, some selflessly dedicated, others little more than dilettantes, who huddled about him. In his diary for 1933 there is an entry calmly appraising his own role:

I cannot speak of the 'indispensability' of my work, even about the period from 1917 to 1921. But now my work is 'indispensable' in the full sense of the word. There is no arrogance in this claim at all. The collapse of the two Internationals [Socialist and Communist after the rise of Hitler] has posed a problem which none of the leaders of these Internationals is at all equipped to solve. The vicissitudes of my personal fate have confronted me with this problem and armed me with important experience in dealing with it. There is now no one except me to carry out the mission of arming a new generation with the revolutionary method over the heads of the leaders of the Second and Third Internationals. And I am in complete agreement with Lenin (or rather Turgenev) that the worst vice is to be more than 55 years old! I need at least about five more years of uninterrupted work to ensure the succession.

With his loyal followers Trotsky was endlessly patient, encouraging, helpful: the banished spokesman for Bolshevik grandeur, the last tutor of the revolution. It is impressive, in reading through Trotsky's collected writings, to see the readiness with which he stole time from major works in order to discuss and correspond with a vast range of people, from veteran revolutionists to casual *nudniks*. But it was all to no avail. The man and the moment did not meet, perhaps they never could again. Among the scattered but slowly growing left-wing and anti-Stalinist groups Trotsky won more admiration than adherence, even the victims of his scorching polemics occasionally taking a wry sort of pleasure in his gift for argument. To Trotsky this could have brought little gratification: a man intent upon transforming history is not to be consoled by praise for his style.

6   Final Legacy

The most enduring portion of Trotsky's writings composed in his years of exile was not directly polemical or even narrowly political. It was directed to the world at large rather than the isolated sects of anti-Stalinist radicalism; it represents the culminating achievement of a major twentieth-century writer for whom the bitterness of defeat and the sufferings of persecution nevertheless brought an opportunity to fulfil his talent. The major books of these last eleven or twelve years are Trotsky's autobiography, *My Life*, the lyrical fragment on Lenin's youth, the severely controlled biography of Stalin, the masterful compression of his basic views on Stalinism called *The Revolution Betrayed*, and, above all, *The History of the Russian Revolution*.

Written very soon after Trotsky began his exile in Turkey, *My Life* seems strongest in its first few chapters, rapid sketches of childhood, school and early radicalism. In the very first paragraph Trotsky sets himself, with the self-consciousness of a seriously ambitious writer, against a major tradition of Russian literature: those spacious recollections of youth and portrayals of idyllic country life one finds in Aksakov, Tolstoy and Turgenev. But far from simply yielding himself to these predecessors, Trotsky strikes at the outset a note of respectful challenge, for he is after all a revolutionist:

The idealization of childhood originated in the literature of the privileged. A secure, affluent and unclouded childhood, spent in a home of inherited wealth and culture, a childhood of affection and play, brings back to one memories of a sunny meadow at the beginning of the road of life. The grandees of literature, or the plebeians who glorify the grandees, have canonized this purely aristocratic view of childhood. But the majority of the people, if it looks back at all, sees, on the contrary, a childhood of darkness, hunger and dependence. Life strikes the weak – and who is weaker than a child?

Yet the tradition of 'the grandees' is not to be dismissed so readily, not even by the revolutionist who helped destroy it; the early pages of *My Life* are rich with echoes of classical Russian literature, abounding with a serenity of space and air, an affection for the little things of daily existence, an immersion in the world of the senses that is rare in the Marxist canon. Trotsky writes, for example, about his childhood on his father's farm in a style that shows how well he remembered, and learned from, 'the literature of the privileged':

> The barns, divided into bins, held fresh-smelling wheat, rough-prickly barley, smooth, almost liquid flaxseed, the blue-black beads of the winter rape, and light, slender oats. When the children played at hide-and-seek, they were allowed, on occasions when there were special guests, to hide in the barns. Crawling over one of the partitions into a bin, I would scramble up the mound of wheat and slip down on the other side. My arms would be buried to the elbows and my legs to the knees in the sliding mass of wheat, and my shirt and shoes, too often torn, would be filled with grain . . .

The political sections of *My Life* lack the vividness of these early chapters, perhaps because Trotsky is covering ground that he has already touched upon in earlier books and expects to deal with more authoritatively in later ones. There are snapshots, often witty and malicious, of leading figures in the European Social Democracy; but about Stalin, still treated mistakenly as a mere bureaucratic mediocrity, and the significance of Stalinism as a social phenomenon, *My Life* offers interpretations that, when compared with the books to come, seem rudimentary. About Trotsky's inner life, his private feelings, his relations with women and children, the book is stringently reticent, for he regards himself as a political man, he is writing a public autobiography, and the very thought of spilling out revelations would have been repugnant to him. Composed a little too early in his life, when some major elements of his thought had not yet crystallized, *My Life* suffers from a fault perhaps characteristic of the public autobiography : it is neither quite a personal narrative nor a comprehensive public record but alternates with brilliant uncertainty between the two.

The History of the Russian Revolution, an enormous three-volume work composed in thirteen months under the trying conditions of exile, is surely Trotsky's masterpiece, the single greatest work of history in the Marxist vein. Marxist not only in its terms of perception, so that the narrative unfolds as a great drama of the struggle between classes, but above all in its insistence that the mute objects of Russian oppression, the masses of proletarians and peasants, have now become active subjects, forging their own destiny on the streets, in the shops, and across the countryside. At times the masses are submitted to cool and dispassionate examination, shown in molecular drift, still more a potential of historical will than a cohered, purposeful force; at other times they take on an almost legendary strength, as if they have become a collective person, bound by class consciousness into a unity of power. Marxism serves here both as analytical method and political myth, a way of understanding and a way of transforming history. Later, Trotsky would pride himself on the claim that while the book was, of course, open to political and intellectual challenge, no serious errors of fact had been detected by its critics – even though he was forced, in Turkey, to write without access to libraries. He had tried, he said in the preface to the book, to be 'objective' without pretending to be 'impartial', and for once this seems really a distinction pointing to a difference.

The History is a work on the grand scale, epic in tone and proportion, brilliant in verbal colouring, quick with the passions of strongly remembered events. One sign of its superiority to *My Life*, which on a smaller scale also tells the story of the revolution, is that the piquant detail, the sardonic stroke, the brilliant summary characterizations are now firmly placed into a commanding structure. The great fault of Trotsky's earlier writing – bravura display for its own sake – is all but gone. *The History* is a work of high self-consciousness, parts tightly aligned with an eye towards a pattern of mosaic, incidents figured on behalf of an aura of inevitability.

The sharp, scornful sentences one has come to expect from Trotsky are there, of course. Chernov, the SR leader : 'abstention from voting became for him a form of political life'. Kerensky : 'not a revolutionist; he merely hung around the revolution' indulging 'the kind of eloquence which operates neither upon mind nor will, but upon the nerves'. Martov : 'The moment when the balance is still oscillating is his moment – this inventive statesman of eternal waverings.' Lenin upon his return to Russia in 1917 : 'he endured the flood of eulogistic speeches like an impatient pedestrian waiting in a doorway for the rain to stop'. The masses : 'A revolution is always distinguished by impoliteness, probably because the ruling classes did not take the trouble in good season to teach the people fine manners.'

Trotsky's tone is supremely self-confident, sometimes openly arrogant : it registers the voice of an *assured* victor. His strategy as narrator is to aim not for suspense but an expected fulfilment. Trenchant observations and wicked thrusts : these are now at the bidding of ideology, or more accurately, of an epic narrative being shaped in accord with that ideology.

I use the term 'epic' intending more than an approximate suggestion of narrative sweep, heroic action, large consequence. I mean it to indicate that the book follows the curve of traditional epic narrative, not, probably, with deliberate intent or plan, but as a consequence of the sheer magnitude of the task Trotsky set himself. The formation of a people, a great theme of the epic, becomes in Trotsky's book the emergence of a new historical epoch; the forging of nationhood becomes the breakthrough of the proletariat into self-awareness; and the testing of a hero becomes the steeling of the revolutionary party.

In still another way does *The History* resemble the epic :

it ends on a note of fulfilment and high optimism. That the world has learned to recognize such terms as Bolshevik and Soviet, writes Trotsky in his concluding sentence, 'alone justifies the proletarian revolution, if you imagine that it needs justification'. One has to remind oneself that the man writing these lines is an exile who in his book has refused that option of tragedy which carrying his story just a little further in time might entail. The epic tells of the early glory, not the later decline, of Rome; so too with Trotsky's account of the revolution. The choice of genre seems to reflect a world-view or, perhaps, a decision to maintain that world-view at all odds. In *The History* the epic 'hero' appears as the aroused maker of history shifting readily through three appearances: the newly triumphant proletariat, the newly triumphant party, the newly triumphant Lenin. Each, so to say, stands in for the other: the proletariat the arm of history, the party the fist of the proletariat, Lenin the brain of the party. At least until the next breakdown into a dialectic of struggle, history seems here well arranged, working according to plan, ending in a synthesis of triumph. For readers suspicious of visions or narratives clamped into excessive order, all this may constitute a certain sleight of hand; among later historians, this schema of necessary unfoldment has been a major ground for criticizing Trotsky's version of the revolution.

The tone is that of the epic too: grand, soaring, assertive, all but wilfully brushing aside the knowledge writer and reader share about what is to happen after the last page. Only the writer at the crest of victory, or determined to remember how it felt to be there, can long maintain this voice of historical exhilaration. Here, in a passage worthy of Dickens, is how Trotsky evokes St Petersburg on the eve of revolution:

All is changed and yet all remains as before. The revolution has shaken the country, deepened the split, frightened some, embittered others, but not yet wiped out a thing or replaced it. Imperial St Petersburg seems drowned in a sleepy lethargy rather than dead. The revolution has stuck little red flags in the hands of the cast-iron monuments of the monarchy.

Great red streamers are hanging down the fronts of the government buildings. But the palaces, the ministries, the headquarters, seem to be living a life entirely apart from those red banners, tolerably faded, moreover, by the autumn rains. The two-headed eagles with the sceptre of empire have been torn down where possible, but oftener draped or hastily painted over. They seem to be lurking there. All the old Russia is lurking, its jaws set in rage.

During the insurrection itself there is uncertainty about storming the Peter and Paul Fortress:

The uncertainty lies in a bicycle battalion. Recruited, like the cavalry, from well-to-do and rich peasants, the bicycle men, coming from the intermediate city layers, constituted a most conservative part of the army. A theme for idealistic psychologists: Let a man find himself, in distinction from others, on top of two wheels with a chain – at least in a poor country like Russia – and his vanity begins to swell out like his tyres. In America it takes an automobile to produce this effect.

And earlier in the book, the workers from the radical Vyborg district come out on the Sampsonievsky Prospect, there to encounter a troop of Cossacks: the fate of the revolution seems to hang on this symbolic meeting.

. . . the horsemen, cautiously, in a long ribbon, rode through the corridor just made by the officers. 'Some of them smiled,' Kayurov [a worker Bolshevik] recalls, 'and one of them gave the workers a good wink.' This wink was not without meaning. The workers were emboldened with a friendly, not hostile, kind of assurance, and slightly infected the Cossacks with it. The one who winked found imitators. In spite of renewed efforts from the officers, the Cossacks, without openly breaking discipline, failed to force the crowd to disperse, but flowed through it in streams . . . Individual Cossacks began to reply to the workers' questions and even to enter into momentary conversations with them. Of discipline there remained but a thin transparent shell that threatened to break through any second. The officers hastened to separate their patrol from the workers, and, abandoning the idea of dispersing them, lined the Cossacks out across the street as a barrier to prevent the demonstrators from getting to the centre. But even this did not help: standing stock-still in perfect discipline, the Cossacks did not hinder the workers from 'diving' under their horses. The revolution did not choose its paths: it made its first steps towards victory under the belly of a Cossack's horse.

Epic but also idyllic. By the late twenties and early thirties the Bolsheviks, staggering under problems and failures, sometimes oppressed by their own handiwork, and more fearful of one another than they had ever been of the Tsarist police, were inclined to look back upon the October revolution almost as a time of innocence: the good, the great days. Trotsky's is pre-lapsarian history, or a simulation of it. And it is not hard to imagine that the more reflective among his enemies, huddling nervously in the Kremlin, would secretly turn to *The History* in order to share with its author a return to the 'idyll' of their past.' Later readers, still susceptible to the sonorities of October, would no doubt experience a similar need to relish the story unstained by denouement. Its sophistication notwithstanding, *The History* is not a book that shares the taste for the anxious and the problematic which has come to dominate serious thought in our century.

Still another literary comparison suggests itself: a comparison with myth. *The History* tells the story of the Russian Revolution as an unfolding and vindication of Bolshevik myth, which does not necessarily mean that it is untrue, only that it seems more persuasive as a work of imagination than of critical history. It is a book that ascends ineluctably from its own premises, everything hinged on the idea of necessity, every paragraph contributing towards a rush of fulfilment. With each page the aura of inevitability thickens. This is not, of course, something that can be maintained for three volumes without a break, and contradictions and doubts do sometimes show themselves. Trotsky is honest enough, for example, to face the question – would the revolution have succeeded if by chance Lenin had been killed a few months earlier? His answer is a gingerly no, it probably would not have succeeded, so central was the role of *this* individual. Yet this is only an intellectual recognition, and it does not crucially interfere with the upward rhythm of the narrative. The book moves ahead steadily, inexorably: history's guardian. Because it acts in accord with the 'agenda' of history, just as the epic hero acted in accord with the command of the gods, the triad of Progress – class/party/leader – reaches victory in a blaze of certainty. Anyone who surrenders himself even a little to Trotsky's narrative powers must find this story exhilarating, but a critical intelligence is likely to want stops for question and debate, likely to suspect that the actuality was more chaotic than Trotsky allows.

Of the problematic, the doubting, the hesitant, the tragic: of all these elements of the human enterprise *The History* has little to say, except when it turns for a glance at the vanquished and then mainly to dismiss them as the refuse of history. There are great chapters on the sociology of dual power and the strategy of insurrection, but those who might look for reflection about the human lot, some touches of insight into the nature of mankind, are not likely to find them here. The power of mind in *The History*, and it is a very great power, is not of the kind that consorts with traditional modes of wisdom.

As historian Trotsky lacks the austere dispassionateness of Thucydides, the sense of watching a great action from a distance such that all human desire shrinks in scale and all human partisanship melts to transience. This, Trotsky would be the first to say, is precisely the kind of history he wishes not to write, a history of 'wisdom' and resignation. He writes from another perspective, that of the embroiled participant who cannot, indeed would not, choose the detachment of tragedy.

By the same token, it can be said that Trotsky, unlike other great historians, refuses to grant his opponents dignity, and except perhaps with regard to Martov, hardly shows them respect. Again Trotsky might answer: who among these opponents had much dignity or merited much respect? The vain and hysterical Kerensky? The leaders of Menshevism who had missed their chance to bring Russia the social changes they knew it yearned for? The White Guard generals, some brave enough, but utterly uncomprehending of the historical storm that had swept them aside? Trotsky's tone of ironic contempt is a consequence not just of personal imperiousness or Bolshevik certitude, but also of a thought-out verdict upon those who had been defeated. Whether this corresponds to our deepest sense of the human situation, or satisfies the greatest possibilities open to the historian, is another question. For even the reader prepared to yield himself to the triumphant absolutism with which *The History* moves towards its climax, will sooner or later remember that its author too was one of the defeated.

How intransigent he remained in defeat! To have come even briefly under his influence during the 1930s was to learn a lesson in moral courage. It was to learn the satisfaction of standing firm by one's convictions, to realize that life offers far worse things than being in a minority. This was not perhaps the lesson that Trotsky meant primarily to teach, but it was a good one.

Straining against the barriers which the host governments of Norway and France put up against him, Trotsky worked with a relentless energy, sometimes eighteen hours a day, to refute the barrage of slanders that now kept coming out of the Moscow trials. Forty years later it may be needless to provide much detail about this gruesome charade, since everyone knows the trials were staged frame-ups. But in the mid-1930s, when so many Bolshevik leaders – Zinoviev, Kamenev, Rakovsky, Radek, Pyatakov, Bukharin – shamed themselves by 'confessing' to incredible crimes, not least that they had conspired with Nazi Germany, Trotsky had to strain every nerve and marshal all his personal resources to cope with the world-wide system of falsehood the Stalinist parties had created. Their propaganda was often aided by liberals who had come to admire the Soviet Union only after it had entered its totalitarian phase and by conservatives delighted with the 'discipline' the Kremlin dictator exacted. It is a sad comment on our age that throughout the world large numbers of distinguished writers and intellectuals rushed to the defence of the dictatorship, finding both crude and subtle reasons to endorse the trials.

Fighting for his political honour, shaken by the sight of old comrades lending themselves to the humiliation of the show trials, Trotsky kept up a stream of exposure and refutation, catching out the organizers of the trials in contradiction and falsehood. He publicly challenged the Russian government to propose his extradition; the challenge was not accepted. To a public meeting in New York he sent a message:

> I am ready to appear before a public and impartial Commission of Enquiry with documents, facts, and testimonies . . . If this commission decides that I am guilty in the slightest degree of the crimes which Stalin imputes to me, I pledge in advance to place myself voluntarily in the hands of the executioners of the GPU . . . But, if the Commission establishes – do you hear me? do you hear me? – that the Moscow Trials are a conscious and premeditated frame-up, I will not ask my accusers to place themselves voluntarily before a firing squad . . . Do the accusers in the Kremlin hear me? I throw my defiance in their faces, and I await their reply.

When Trotsky heard that his old political friend, Angelica Balabanoff, had grown depressed because of the Moscow trials, he wrote to her in 1937: 'Indignation, anger, revulsion? Yes, even temporary weariness. All this is human, only too human. But I will not believe that you have succumbed to pessimism . . . History has to be taken as she is; and when she allows herself such extraordinary and filthy outrages, one must fight her back with one's fists.'

Human, only too human, he himself certainly was. Natalya Trotsky, in her memoirs, recalls that when her husband was alone in his study

I sometimes heard him heave a deep sigh and say to himself, 'I am tired, so tired. I can't take any more.' He would never have admitted it openly. The senseless humiliation, the moral collapse of old revolutionaries who had loved him and yet had died covering him and themselves with obloquy, filled him with inconsolable anguish.

One question nagged incessantly at Trotsky, as later at many others: how could these men, old revolutionists who had shown courage in the prisons of the Tsars and some of whom had fought fearlessly in the civil war, now permit themselves to be publicly shamed? There was no certain or single answer, and probably there still is not. We know that some of the Old Bolsheviks had been progressively demoralized by the regime, so that by the time of the trials they were broken men; we know that some were threatened with the death of close relatives and that others had themselves been tortured; we know that some were promised remission of sentences, and perhaps other secret arrangements, if they submitted to Stalin's will. And there are theories, still by no means validated, that some of them, in their grief and demoralization, had been persuaded that false confessions would be the last 'contribution' they could make to the revolution. But none of these explanations seems fully satisfying, perhaps because in an age of totalitarianism the mind, clinging to some last margin of rationality, cannot bring itself to accept what the eye sees.

It was, finally, a great relief to Trotsky when the Joint Commission of Enquiry, consisting of intellectuals and veteran radicals overwhelmingly his political opponents, opened its hearings in Mexico City in April 1937. The Commission was headed by the aged American philosopher John Dewey, who had put aside a study of logic in order to undertake what he regarded as his moral obligation. For a full week Trotsky answered questions, not only in regard to the trials themselves but also about his entire political career. Many of the questions were politically hostile, especially those concerning the relation between Bolshevism and Stalinism; the record of the hearings, printed as *The Case of Leon Trotsky*, contains absorbing

pages of political and intellectual exchange between
Trotsky and such critical interlocutors as John Dewey,
Benjamin Stolberg, Otto Ruehle and the Commission's
Counsel, John Finerty.[1] Throughout the hearings Trotsky
spoke in English, a language in which he was not quite at
home, but despite lapses and misconstructions, he spoke
well. His speech of summation constitutes both a recollec-
tion of his political life and a demolition of the trials. It
ends with this credo:

> The experiences of my life, in which there has been no
> lack of either success or failures, has not only not destroyed
> my faith in the clear, bright future of mankind, but, on
> the contrary, has given it an indestructible temper. This
> faith in reason, in truth, in human solidarity, which at the
> age of eighteen I took with me into the workers' quarters
> of the provincial town of Nikolayev – this faith I have
> preserved fully and completely. It has become more mature,
> but not less ardent.

The Commission declared Trotsky 'Not Guilty', but this
had rather little effect on public opinion at the time,
especially in European intellectual circles.

Precisely the revulsion from Stalinism that a rather small
but significant minority of Western intellectuals was now
experiencing, led it to question Trotsky's premise that there
was a deep conflict, a fundamental discontinuity between
Bolshevism and Stalinism. Anti-Stalinist, left-wing intellectuals who had been impressed by Trotsky's theories –
indeed, had often been prodded by his writings into
abandoning 'progressivist' illusions about Stalinism – often
concluded that he did not go far enough. They concluded
that he had too much at stake in defending his own past
as a Bolshevik leader, or that his ideological rigidities
prevented him from undertaking a sufficiently comprehensive criticism of the whole political and moral outlook
which, they suspected, Stalinism shared with Leninism.
In an ambitious essay, 'Their Morals and Ours', Trotsky
turned to this issue with both combativeness and

impatience – the combativeness of a seasoned Marxist polemicist, the impatience of a Russian revolutionist who feels that in answering critics like Max Eastman, Boris Souvarine and Victor Serge he must repeat what had been said conclusively decades earlier in reply to Russian ex-Marxists.

In 'Their Morals and Ours' Trotsky argues that moral standards are historically relative, certainly that they are historically conditioned; tries to show the social causes of the moral distance between Leninism and Stalinism; reiterates his defence of the methods employed by the Bolshevik regime; and has little difficulty in demonstrating that his liberal and social democratic critics are necessarily quite as committed as they charge he is to the view that 'the end justifies the means'. What is more, this holds for all shades of political opinion, except primitive Christians, absolute pacifists, and other precursors and disciples of Kantianism. In the less polemical sections of this essay, Trotsky struggles with the vexing problems of the relation between historically conditioned moral values, as these reflect the interests of social classes, and those moral absolutes he was inclined to depreciate as excessively abstract but which he nevertheless found it impossible to avoid invoking himself. The most valuable and sophisticated portion of 'Their Morals and Ours' analyses the inter-relationship between means and ends, how the two shift place with the passage of events – in effect, an argument against any simple or stark dualism.

Anticipating the obvious rejoinder to his claim that 'morality is a product of social development' and 'that there is nothing immutable about it', Trotsky writes:

> But do not elementary moral precepts exist, worked out in the development of humanity as a whole and indispensable for the existence of every collective body? Undoubtedly such precepts exist but the extent of their action is extremely limited and unstable. Norms 'obligatory upon all' become the less forceful the sharper the character assumed by the class struggle.

Trotsky then proceeds to a lively defence of 'Bolshevik amoralism', especially the Decree of 1919 which allowed the Red Army to take as hostages relatives of army commanders suspected of uncertain loyalty. 'It was a necessary measure in the struggle against the oppressors.' Wherein, then, is this policy different from the Stalinist taking of hostages (children and wives of Oppositionists) which Trotsky attacked so bitterly? 'Only in the historical context of the struggle lies the justification of the [1919] Decree as in general the justification of the whole civil war which, too, can be called, not without foundation, "disgusting barbarism".' Still – it may be in deference to those 'elementary moral precepts' which Trotsky holds to be 'extremely limited and unstable' – he feels obliged to add that 'the Decree of 1919 led scarcely to even one execution . . .' Nor does he try to deny that in the civil war both sides indulged in 'disgusting barbarism' – for the unpleasant but unavoidable truth is that 'armies in combat are always more or less symmetrical; were there nothing in common in their methods of struggle they could not inflict blows upon each other'.

Trotsky, then, has no trouble in showing how often his critics are inconsistent or guilty of high-minded cant. Victor Serge, for example, indignant about the taking of hostages by the Bolsheviks during the civil war, charged Trotsky with believing, in effect, that it was permissible for his side to use such methods but deplorable when his enemies used them. This same Victor Serge, notes Trotsky in reply, joined the POUM in the Spanish Civil War, 'a Catalan party which had its own militia at the front . . . At the front, as is well known, people shoot and kill. It may therefore be said : "For Victor Serge killings assume entirely different meaning depending upon whether the order is issued by General Franco or by the leaders of Serge's own party." '

The same point would presumably hold with regard to other historical events. The Second World War, judged by liberals and socialists as a necessary undertaking to defeat Hitlerism, included actions morally deplorable in their own right, e.g. firebombing German cities and dropping atomic bombs on Hiroshima and Nagasaki, with the resulting death of tens of thousands of innocent civilians. Insofar as these actions could be justified at all, it was primarily through some version of the argument that 'the end justifies the means' – for what else but a proximate end (the defeat of the Axis in the shortest possible time and with the fewest casualties) *could* justify such dreadful means? Those who did offer justifications for such acts (not all of them : some people argued, for example, that it was not necessary to drop the second H-bomb) found themselves using arguments quite similar to those of Trotsky's 'Bolshevik amoralism'. With one difference : Trotsky was usually more honest in facing up to the costs of historical action.

What, then, is the end that in Trotsky's view could justify the means employed by the Bolsheviks? 'Increasing the power of humanity over nature and . . . the abolition of the power of one person over another', which for him signifies the revolutionary prosecution of the class struggle in order to achieve socialism. Yet, Trotsky stressed, this is not to say that all means are permissible. 'All means are permissible which genuinely lead to mankind's emancipation,' but certain means clearly will not; the means to be used in revolutionary struggle must 'impart solidarity and unity to revolutionary workers . . . which imbue them with the consciousness of their historic tasks . . . Consequently, not *all* means are permissible.' During the civil war the Bolsheviks had not hesitated to lie in order to mislead their military opponents, just as Abraham Lincoln had not hesitated during the civil war in America; but, continues Trotsky, the Bolsheviks had been truthful in what they said to the workers. Even these criteria 'do not, of course, give a ready answer to the question as to what is permissible and what is not permissible in each separate case. There can be no such automatic answers.' Judgement, intelligence, experience, risk : these are necessary.

For all its power, especially in devastating easy moral righteousness, Trotsky's argument contains serious difficulties :

1. In responding to the vicious conduct of the Stalinist

regime, he found himself resorting spontaneously and passionately to the kind of humanitarian or supra-class moralism that he dismissed on other occasions. He wrote, not just about the reactionary drift of Stalinism, but also about its 'baseness' and 'perfidy' – terms taken from the traditional moral lexicon and implying a preference for their opposites, 'nobility' and 'integrity'. The 'elementary moral precepts' he had found to be 'extremely limited and unstable' now played a strikingly large role in his battle against the Stalinist dictatorship. Repeatedly he charged it, in effect, with violating that 'moral sense' which his essay tended to minimize. Just as Trotsky could show that in extreme circumstances the liberal moralists had no recourse but to justify their conduct with the same maxim that he did, so they could reply that in other extreme circumstances he fell back upon their moral vocabulary and moral emotions. One reason for the effectiveness of his attacks upon Stalinism was precisely that he did so. The deep human need to make moral judgements proved stronger than Marxist qualms about making them.

2. To show that for all but Christian and pacifist absolutists historical action necessarily requires the defence that 'the end justifies the means'., was not yet to cope with the underlying and serious complaint which Trotsky's critics were trying to articulate – namely, that by invoking the 'ultimate end' of socialism, Bolshevism had allowed itself too readily the use of deplorable means for which there was in fact neither immediate need nor probable justification, and which regularly led to consequences detrimental to the goal of socialism. What matters in the choice of means is not just the large proclaimed end, almost always some attractive idea like socialism or democracy, but the probable consequence, the next likely end in the chain of means-and-ends. And what is needed as a check upon human arrogance or vanguard presumption is some standard of judgement, say, an envisioned proximate end open to test or verification, that is closer to living actuality than the utopia of a classless society. Thus, the outlawing of the other socialist parties after the revolution was justified by the Bolsheviks in the name

of the ultimate end of socialism; but the predictable consequences of driving Martov away in 1923 was the rigidification of the regime, the loss of what fragments of democracy still remained – anti-socialist consequences.

This point was nicely developed in a brief but trenchant comment that John Dewey wrote about Trotsky's essay. Dewey distinguished between two common uses of the term 'end' – 'the final justifying end and ends that are themselves means to this final end'. Insofar as the end signifies 'consequences actually reached, it is clearly dependent upon the means used . . . [But] an end-in-view [or a "final justifying end"] represents or is an *idea* of the final consequences . . . a means for directing action – just as a man's *idea* of health to be attained or a house to be built is not identical with *end* in the sense of actual outcome.' What has given a bad name to the maxim that 'the end justifies the means', adds Dewey, is that 'the end-in-view' is commonly employed to justify certain means, *'and so justifies the latter that it is not necessary to examine what the actual consequences of the use of chosen means will be'*. (Emphasis added.)

One could thus make a distinction between the deplorable means employed by the early Bolsheviks that *might* be defensible on the ground of likely immediate consequences (defeat of the White armies) and deplorable means that are not defensible, even though they are justified in the name of the ultimate end of socialism. What is wanted, then, by Dewey and other critics, is a more stringent relationship between means and ends, a severe recognition of their mutual shaping, and a far greater scepticism about invoking 'ultimate ends' as the justification for deplorable actions. To be sure, those engaged in such actions could readily shift the ground of their justification from ultimate end to immediate consequence, but at the very least their task of justification would then be made more difficult.

3. The problem with which both Trotsky and his critics were wrestling is that of the inevitable contamination, and thereby perhaps the inescapable tragedy, of all human action. Not to act may be to acquiesce in the intolerable;

to act is to risk consequences unforeseen and often alloyed by the means necessary for effective action; rarely if ever can there be a complete moral harmony between means and ends. Trotsky of course chooses the Promethean option, and his ethical bias depends in good part on his ideological insistence upon seeing most of human conduct, especially political conduct, through the imagery of conflict, often the imagery of civil war, in which 'elementary moral precepts' must be slackened or abandoned. This is the strategy he employs in 'Their Morals and Ours', and since he is obviously right in saying that 'moral precepts' do not survive very well under conditions of civil war, he makes it hard for his critics to endow their moral criticism with an air of realism. Still, even in the twentieth century, human existence cannot be reduced to the starkness of civil war, nor moral consciousness to the exigencies forced upon combatants in civil war. In the Soviet Union, after the civil war, there came a time of relative social peace in which traditional problems of society and politics reasserted themselves. Age-old problems of politics – representation, bureaucracy, diffusion of power, corruption – had to be confronted anew, as did age-old problems of public morality – the restraints imposed on rulers to avoid reducing political life to a state of terror, the appropriate relations between those who wield and those who submit to power, the terms by which the authority of a state may be justified, etc. These were problems which could not readily be dealt with in the ultimatistic terms that Trotsky used in his essay, just as they could not readily be dealt with by the kind of politics the Bolsheviks practised.

Perhaps the trouble here has to do with a certain mode of Marxist thought. Throughout Trotsky's essay there is a frequent resort, explicitly or not, to the notion of 'the last analysis' – as one might say, 'in the last analysis the state is the executive committee of the ruling class', or as in the tendency to see democracy as 'mere bourgeois democracy', a fault of which so keen a mind as Trotsky could also be guilty. For even if 'in the last analysis' politics is nothing more than a disguised or unacknowledged version of civil war, and even if 'in the last analysis' bourgeois democracy signifies nothing more than the domination of a ruling class, there is still much to be experienced and understood before reaching that 'last analysis'. To this crucial area of social existence Trotsky would not give sufficient political or moral credence: society was almost always, for him, either moving towards or retreating from revolution. The moral arguments that his critics directed against Bolshevism had as their urgent if not always well-articulated premise a conviction drawn from the terrible events of our century: that democracy, call it 'bourgeois democracy' if you wish, is absolutely essential for the political life of both socialists and non-socialists and that any view of political morality which denies this must be radically deficient.

Some such tacit criticism would seem to lie behind Dewey's point that in 'Their Morals and Ours' Trotsky tends to absolutize the class struggle, and the Bolshevik version of class struggle at that, as 'the only means' towards socialism. 'The belief that a law of history determines the particular way in which the struggle is to be carried on', notes Dewey, 'certainly seems to tend towards a fanatical and even mystical devotion to use of certain ways of conducting the class struggle . . .' Dewey concludes that 'in avoiding one kind of absolutism Mr Trotsky has plunged into another kind of absolutism'. What Dewey calls 'the class struggle' evidently refers here to the whole Bolshevik conception of politics: that which Trotsky, notwithstanding his high intelligence, refused to put into question.

One of the matters about which Trotsky did begin to show greater intellectual flexibility was the Jewish question. Most of his life he had cleaved faithfully to the orthodox Marxist line: that the basic solution to such problems as anti-Semitism, discrimination and Jewish economic 'abnormality' lay in socialism; that the Zionist idea was a nationalist utopia, unrealizable under capitalism, unnecessary beyond it; and that the 'separatism' of the Bund, the Jewish socialist movement of Poland combining Marxist politics with cultural Yiddishism, was to be opposed

vigorously, since Jewish radicals ought to join the movements of the countries in which they live and not isolate
themselves in left-wing ghettoes. In the early years of the
century Trotsky had been especially violent in attacking
the Bund as an agent of heresy, and its leaders had in turn
regarded him with greater distaste than they felt for most
of the other Russian Marxists. Otherwise, he had not said
or done anything very notable with regard to the Jews or
Jewishness. Like a good many Russian Marxists of Jewish
origin, he evidently felt a strong desire, arising out of both
political conviction and more obscure personal feelings, to
take the path of complete assimilation. For most of his
life, in fact, he behaved as if he were completely assimi-
lated, denying the significance of 'Jewish identity' and
finding in his revolutionary role enough substance for self-
definition. Some of his biographers have speculated that,
wish it or not, he must still have remembered a few scraps
of Yiddish from childhood; if so, he took care not to flaunt
them before the world.

In the 1930s, we learn from a scholarly monograph by
Joseph Nedava, Trotsky began to display a surprising
interest in the Jewish settlement in Palestine, especially
its labour movement. Nedava cites a little-known memoir
by Hersch Mendl, a Polish-Jewish Trotskyist, who in 1934
held a lengthy discussion with Trotsky on these topics in
Paris. Trotsky asked for material on recent events in
Palestine, and

I immediately wrote about [this] request to my comrades
in Poland, but I soon forgot all about it. From the history
of the international movement I had known of a number
of Jewish revolutionaries who had from time to time
recalled the fact that they belonged to the Jewish people
but soon forgot this fact. I thought that this would happen
in this instance too. But Trotsky was not one of those who
forget things that they consider important. Not only did he
not forget but, as was his manner, he even drew the com-
pelling conclusion – not consistent to the end, but quite
radical – when he declared, at the beginning of World
War II, that Jews were entitled to a country of their own.

In 1937, after his arrival in Mexico, Trotsky expressed himself with considerable openness:

> During my youth I rather leaned towards the prognosis that the Jews of different countries would be assimilated and that the Jewish question would thus disappear, as it were, automatically. The historical development of the last quarter of a century has not confirmed this view. Decaying capitalism has everywhere swung over to an intensified nationalism, one aspect of which is anti-Semitism. The Jewish question has loomed largest in the most highly developed capitalist country of Europe, Germany.

Since one could no longer expect the Jewish problem to be solved by the automatic process of assimilation, Trotsky now spoke, without evident irony, about something that few orthodox Marxists had previously acknowledged: 'a Jewish nation'.

> The Jews of different countries have created their press and developed the Yiddish language as an instrument adapted to modern culture. One must therefore reckon with the fact that the Jewish nation will maintain itself for an entire epoch to come.

To what precise conclusions he wished to bring these stabs at new understanding, we cannot be certain. He continued to regard Zionism as 'incapable of resolving the Jewish question' – and for a reason that now seems anying but irrelevant: 'The conflict between the Jews and Arabs in Palestine acquires a more and more tragic and more and more menacing character.' But at the same time he was toying with the idea of 'great migrations' by 'the dispersed Jews who would want to be reassembled in the same community' – not very far from what would actually happen in a few years. He also believed that British imperialism was still strong enough to thwart the hopes of Zionism. 'The future development of military events', he feared, 'may well transform Palestine into a bloody trap for several hundred thousand Jews.' Clearly he had not yet worked out a consistent point of view; he was struggling towards new insights and speaking with a sympathy about Jewish settlement that went against his past tradition.

Nedava writes that 'one can almost surely assume that under the changed circumstances brought about by the establishment of the state of Israel, in the wake of which great migrations of nationalities also occurred, Trotsky – had he lived to witness the historic event – would have subscribed to the Zionist solution'. I am afraid that one cannot assume anything of the sort. And in any case, how can one know? It is a temptation to suppose that if Trotsky had lived he would have been wise enough to share one's opinions, but it is a temptation that ought strenuously to be resisted. The important point, in any case, is that Trotsky's hesitant and groping statements on the Jewish question indicate a new uncertainty, a feeling that it would no longer do to keep repeating the old 'positions'. He did not have time to think the problem through, other problems concerned him more, and he obviously had no intention of breaking past the limits of his ideology; but there *is* a new awareness, a new sensitiveness.[2]

For Trotsky, as well as for most other people in left-wing anti-Stalinist circles, the major political problem of the century remained 'the Russian question'. How was one to interpret the terrifying developments which each day's wire service reported from Stalinist Russia? Among liberals, then and later, it was a source of merriment to watch the convoluted debates about the nature of Stalinism to which the left-wing groups devoted themselves. These seemed, to the liberals, a perfect example of the hopeless scholasticism of the Marxist mind. But Trotsky was right on this matter, if not in his detailed analysis then in his general preoccupation. Stalinism represented a new, unexplored and tremendously important phenomenon, regardless of whether one saw it as an ultimate fulfilment of Leninism, as (in Trotsky's formula) a 'degenerated workers' state', or as a fearful historical mutation presided over by a 'new class'. The fierce debates on the left during the 1930s were often conducted in the esoteric vocabulary of Marxist factionalism, a kind of secret code that outsiders found almost impossible to break. Sometimes they were conducted with a polemical fury masking a sense of profound intellectual bewilderment. But these were important debates, touching on topics which a new generation of political analysts, both academic and non-academic, would repeat in other languages a few decades later. Let the anti-Stalinist left at least have the bit of credit it deserves for anticipating and grappling with a major historical problem.

In the last two years of his life Trotsky plunged into a discussion concerning the political role and sociological nature of Stalinist Russia which had been provoked by some of his American followers, led by Max Shachtman and James Burnham, who found increasingly unsatisfactory his view that Russia merited 'critical support' in the war because it remained a 'degenerated workers' state'. (About the phrase 'critical support', which agitated both sides in this dispute, there was something unreal: nothing concrete in the way of action was possible to either group, only an opinion as to what should be done if anything could be.) When Russian armies marched into Finland, Trotsky denounced the invasion as another instance of Stalinist reaction, yet because he saw the Russo-Finnish war as part of a larger conflict between the bourgeois West and the Soviet Union, he continued in his writings to give the latter 'critical support'. The dialectical torturousness of this position could hardly solicit much understanding, let alone assent; it reflected, at best, the difficulties of grappling with unforeseen problems.

To the end of his life Trotsky held that Stalinist Russia should still be designated as a 'degenerated workers' state' because it preserved the nationalized property forms that were a 'conquest' of the Russian Revolution. In his view this was a society without an independent historical perspective, one that would soon have to give way to either bourgeois restoration or a new proletarian uprising. For the Stalinist bureaucracy to constitute a new class and the society it ruled to be seen as a new social order, neither capitalist nor socialist, there would have to be a 'virtual liquidation of the planned economy' and of nationalized ownership. And that had not yet occurred. Nevertheless, there seem to be some signs that towards the end of his life Trotsky was, if not abandoning, then seriously modifying his views. In 1939 he wrote, 'The USSR minus the social structure of the October Revolution [nationalized industry and planned economy] would be a Fascist regime.' A cogent enough observation, though how to reconcile a fascist 'superstructure' with the social 'base' of a 'workers' state' is a task that might strain even the most dialectical of minds.

Trotsky's critics, whose views were most fully developed by Shachtman, a gifted American disciple, insisted that the total loss of political power by the Russian working class meant that it no longer ruled in any social sense, indeed, in any real or visible way, for as a propertyless class the proletariat could rule only through political power and not in those indirect ways that the bourgeoisie had been able to employ in its youthful phase. Stalinism, they continued, showed no signs of producing from within itself a bourgeois restoration, and Trotsky had been repeatedly and badly mistaken in supposing he had discovered such signs. Actually, they concluded, the bureaucracy had become a new ruling class, with interests of its own in opposition to both capitalism and socialism. The traditional Marxist dichotomy to which Trotsky clung of capitalism-or-socialism had been shown to be mistaken, perhaps because of the delay or failure of the socialist revolution. Nothing in history 'decreed' such an either/or; there was a third possibility that Shachtman called 'bureaucratic collectivism',[3] a stratified economy dominated by a new ruling class which used totalitarian methods, including large-scale terror, to modernize the backward Russian society through an unprecedented exploitation and to create a powerful new Russian empire. This new society was seen as more reactionary than capitalism, since it deprived the working class of elementary rights which in the Western world had been won in the early nineteenth century. Whether 'bureaucratic collectivism' was a transient phase of Russian development or a possible new social order on a world scale, the dissident Trotskyists did not feel ready to say. The force of their analysis lay more in its rejection of Trotsky's increasingly unpersuasive designation of 'degenerated workers' state' than in their prognosis for the historical future. As it now seems, they were certainly right in insisting upon the historical novelty of the society that had grown up in Russia, one that resembles neither the reality of capitalism nor the idea of socialism; but they did not or could not go very far in developing their own theory of what is signified or what its future might be.

Trotsky argued vigorously against these ideas of his dissident friends, but in one of his last articles, 'The USSR in War', there is a passage notable for openness of mind and an effort to get past mere semantic entanglements:

Our critics have more than once argued that the present Soviet bureaucracy bears very little resemblance to either the bourgeois or labour bureaucracy in capitalist society; that, to a far greater degree than does the fascist bureaucracy, it represents a new and much more powerful social formation. This is quite correct and we have never closed our eyes to it. But if we consider the Soviet bureaucracy a 'class', then we are compelled to state immediately that this class does not at all resemble any of those propertied classes known to us in the past; our gain consequently is not great. We frequently call the Soviet bureaucracy a caste, underscoring thereby its shut-in character, its arbitrary rule, and the haughtiness of the ruling stratum, which considers that its progenitors issued from the divine lips of Brahma whereas the popular masses originated from the grosser portions of his anatomy. But even this definition does not of course possess a strictly scientific character. Its relative superiority lies in this, that the makeshift character of the term is clear to everybody, since it would enter nobody's mind to identify the Moscow oligarchy with the Hindu caste of Brahmins. The old sociological terminology did not and could not prepare a name for a new social event which is in process of evolution (degeneration) and which has not assumed stable forms. All of us, however, continue to call the Soviet bureaucracy a bureaucracy, not being unmindful of its historical peculiarities. In our opinion this should suffice for the time being.

What seems to have troubled Trotsky most about the theoretical revisions proposed by his dissident followers (who in 1940 broke from the Trotskyist movement) was that they called into question the entire revolutionary perspective upon which he continued to base his politics. In this fear he was right, and their protestations to the contrary now seem to have been an evasion. For if the Stalinist bureaucracy represented a new social order that was neither bourgeois nor proletarian, then there was the possibility that its life-span was by no means a brief one and that it could stabilize itself through a mixture of modern repression and modernized economy, holding the masses down but in time giving them a little more bread. There was the further possibility, if Trotsky's critics were right, that the whole perspective of socialism might have to be revised, for while they remained convinced socialists, their theory left open the question of whether the working class could fulfil the tasks assigned to it by Marxism. It might make a revolution, yes; but could it hold power without giving way to a new usurping bureaucracy? Did it have the cohesion, discipline and vision to create a free, humane socialism? Was the débacle of the Soviet Union due to the specific conditions of backward Russia or did it point towards a larger, perhaps even universal tendency? Regarded as heretical in the past, these questions could no longer be suppressed once the dissidents put forward the theory of 'bureaucratic collectivism'.

It is to Trotsky's credit that, even while rejecting such ideas, he was ready at the close of his life to confront the possibility that the proletariat might not fulfil its revolutionary role. In such an event he would have to undertake a fundamental shift in his political thought:

> If this war provokes, as we firmly believe, a proletarian revolution, it must inevitably lead to the overthrow of the bureaucracy in the USSR and the regeneration of Soviet democracy on a far higher economic and cultural basis than

in 1918 ... If, however, it is conceded that the present war will provoke not revolution but a decline of the proletariat, then there remains another alternative: the further decay of monopoly capitalism, its further fusion with the state and the replacement of democracy wherever it still remained by a totalitarian regime. The inability of the proletariat to take into its hands the leadership of society could actually lead under these conditions to the growth of a new exploiting class ...

Because he continued to believe in the either/or of capitalist reaction/socialist revolution, Trotsky ruled out almost entirely the possibility that capitalism might experience a sustained socio-economic revival in a democratic setting. Only in part, therefore, was he right about the consequences of a failure of the proletariat to make the revolution: monopoly capitalism did move closer towards 'fusion with the state', but 'democracy wherever it remained' – which is to say, in the West – was not replaced by 'a totalitarian regime'. Trotsky's apocalyptic vision simply could not encompass the whole ambiguous, unstable, but by no means unhopeful development that we call the welfare state: still capitalist in its socio-economic relations but significantly modified towards greater humaneness, partly as a result of the unbroken power of the working class. Still, if his expectations proved largely mistaken, there is something admirable in his willingness to face up to the possibility that his entire political perspective might have to be abandoned. If so, he saw himself remaining a political actor, but now obligated to develop 'a new minimum programme – to defend the interests of the slaves of the totalitarian bureaucratic system'.

This was a hypothesis to be considered but also to be firmly rejected. To his last day Trotsky held to the Marxist revolutionary idea. With regard to the Second World War, for example, he clung to the Leninist theory of 'imperialist war', which in 1914–17 had told the European working class that it had no stake in either side, the Kaiser's or that of the Western bourgeoisie and the Tsar. Trotsky did of course make some modification in his position on the war : he argued that bourgeois democracy was historically exhausted, that trying to keep it alive would only play into the hands of the fascists and contribute to their victory, that the only way to defeat fascism was to push ahead towards a socialist revolution which would revitalize the masses of Europe and America. All of these arguments tacitly recognized what his formal position failed adequately to acknowledge : there was a deep truth in the feeling of most people that Nazi Germany signified a social evil qualitatively different from, and far greater than, that of traditional capitalism. No wonder Trotsky's views were barely heeded, by either the masses or the socialists, most of the latter concluding that the radically new factor of Hitlerite totalitarianism forced them, with some degree of political criticism, to support the Allied camp. Trotsky's stand on the war had not the slightest practical consequence, and it was just as well.

The last years were difficult. Neither poverty nor power-lessness seemed to trouble him as much as the constricted-ness of his daily existence. In public he remained firm and vigorous; privately he suffered from intervals of depression. Once, it seems, he contemplated suicide. The indignity of needing to defend himself against the slanders pouring out of Moscow, the frustrations he met in trying to rebuild a political movement ('I give advice because I have no other way to act,' he wrote to a friend in France), the annoyance of having to turn out certain articles and books for merely financial reasons, the pain he felt at seeing so many people close to him, including some who had never shared his politics, destroyed by the Stalin regime, the anxiety that he might not live long enough to finish his work – all these left their mark. How could they not? Trotsky was a man of enormous self-discipline, with a firm conviction about his place in history and his responsibility to the idea of socialism; but he was also a complex and sensitive human being, impatient with the turn of history which had left him helpless – only for the moment, he believed – to influence events. In the mid-1930s he kept a diary which reveals flashes of irritation and unhappiness, as if he were rebelling against the disproportion between his intellectual powers and his political opportunities. But the diary also reveals capacities for human warmth and intensity of feeling, especially towards his admirable wife.

Trotsky was only sixty when he was murdered by an agent of the Russian secret police, one 'Jacson' or Ramon Mercador, who had wormed his way into the household by pretending to be a political admirer and the lover of a woman disciple. On 20 August 1940, 'Jacson' came to Trotsky with an article which he said he had written as a reply to the American Trotskyist dissidents on 'the Russian question'; somewhat wearily, since he did not think much of 'Jacson's' political gifts, Trotsky agreed to look it over. The two men went into Trotsky's study, with the assassin nervously clutching his raincoat. As Trotsky bent over the article, 'Jacson' pulled out an ice-axe, closed his eyes, and brought it crashing down on Trotsky's head. The victim let out a terrible cry – 'I shall hear that cry all my life,' the assassin later said. Though his skull was broken and his face bloodied, Trotsky leapt up, hurled ink-pots, books, and then himself at the murderer. People came rushing in; 'Jacson' was beaten by Trotsky's guards; still thinking of political consequences, Trotsky told them not to kill 'Jacson' for 'he must be made to talk'. Natalya held her husband as he slumped to the floor and whispered to her gravely, 'Natasha, I love you.' Taken to a hospital, Trotsky clung to life for another day; a group of surgeons operated on a wound two and three-quarter inches deep. Natalya wrote a few words about her final sight of her husband:

> His head drooped on to his shoulder. The arms fell just as the arms in Titian's 'Descent from the Cross'. Instead of a crown of thorns the dying man wore a bandage. The features of his face retained their purity and pride. It seemed that any moment now he might still straighten up and become his own master again.

But for the killer's blow, the still vigorous Trotsky might

have lived on for a number of years and continued to write and work. It would have been profoundly interesting to see how he would have responded to the political and intellectual problems of the post-war years, when, as it seemed to many people, including some on the left, all political systems had proved to be insufficient. What would have been Trotsky's 'minimum programme to defend the interests of the slaves'? How would he have coped with the fact that while the proletariat failed to make a revolution, nevertheless Europe and America did not sink into fascism? Would he have continued to hold the theory that Russia is 'a degenerated workers' state'? And what would he have said about the splits within the Communist world?

Trotsky's thought could have gone in either of two basic directions, towards a stubborn reassertion of a fundamentalist Bolshevism or towards some problematic version of the socialist idea. We do not know which it would have been, and it seems foolish to suppose that we can. His mind was a mixture of the rigid and the flexible: he held unquestioningly to the basic tenets of Marxism, but within their boundaries he was capable of innovation and risk. The problems he had begun to grapple with in the 1930s were different in kind from those which the dominant minds of his tradition had had to confront; for Trotsky was destined to be the great Marxist witness to the debacle of socialism and the triumph of totalitarianism, events his intellectual mentors had not foreseen. None of the great Marxist figures lived so dramatic a life as he, none with so tragic a conclusion.

There were other problems – already present during the last years of Trotsky's life but visible in their full significance only during the decades since his death – which call into question at least parts of his political outlook. Can the modern phenomenon of totalitarianism, with its vast and systematized irrationalities, its unprecedented structures of terrorism, and its tendency to suppress traditional class dynamics, be understood adequately in terms of Trotsky's Marxism? To be sure, his descriptions and analyses of the genesis of both Stalinism and fascism remain classics of modern political thought, and while they have been improved at various points, it would be a mistake to suppose they have been surpassed. Nevertheless, in part because he did not live to see the terrible denouement of Hitlerism and the final ugliness of Stalinism, Trotsky could not yet cope with the problem, the *idea* of totalitarianism. In his writings of the late 1930s he did begin to use the term 'totalitarian' as a crucial descriptive, but this seems to have referred more to the outer character of Nazi or Stalinist politics than to a new historical phenomenon of major significance. He can hardly be blamed for not having worked out a theory about something which few other analysts had even begun to grapple with, and which still has not found its Marx or Weber; but to have done that, one suspects, he would have had to break past the limits of traditional Marxism or at least stretch them in ways that Marxists had rarely undertaken in the past. There is, to be sure, the suggestive formula, 'socialism or barbarism', which he, together with other Marxists, used in discussing the future of mankind; but it is in the very nature of the alternative he posited that the 'barbarism' could not be detailed, since it betokened depths of brutality the rational imagination could not foresee. That Trotsky acknowledged such a possibility at a time when a good many thinkers, both liberal and socialist, contented themselves with panglossian delusions, is testimony to the strength of his political imagination; whether the 'barbarism' that actually came about in our century could be adequately analysed with the categories of Marxism is another question. I do not think it could be.

Or again: could the murder of six million Jews in Europe be satisfactorily explained through Trotsky's theory that Nazism represented the last brutal attempt by the German bourgeoisie to retain power? No doubt, the big bourgeoisie played a crucial part in the rise of Hitler to power, but it is hard to see that their, or any other, class interests were significantly at stake in Auschwitz and Buchenwald. Perhaps Trotsky would have said that bourgeois decay had reached a point so extreme that rational calculations were no longer in effect, and that all the gathered violence and hatred of the petty bourgeoisie, the declassed intellectuals, and the *lumpen* scum which formed the Nazi movement was now breaking out into a climax of 'barbarism'. Perhaps he would even have acknowledged that this outburst of horror had acquired an autonomous character, long since cut loose from whatever class interests had helped set it into motion. We do not know.

Similarly, and most important of all, with the problem of democracy. Trotsky was extremely sensitive to the decay of European democracy during the years between the two world wars, and his writings on Germany, France and Spain often register brilliantly the ways in which the crisis of capitalist economy endangered the survival of democracy. But the 'class analysis' of democracy, as Trotsky practised it, seems not at all sufficient for an era in which it has become painfully clear that freedom and liberty – far from being mere guises or transient luxuries of class domination – must be taken as the most precious values of modern society.

Staying within the limits of Trotsky's ideology, it would be difficult to account for the considerable stability and the marked rise in living standards that have characterized Western capitalism and now call into question the whole revolutionary perspective. His disciples, in the manner customary to Marxists, have argued that Trotsky erred not in his basic analysis, only in his predictions of the tempo of social collapse. For even if what we are now living through does not quite approximate the 'death agony of capitalism', it is still possible that the crises Trotsky foresaw have merely been delayed. By its very nature, this argument cannot be refuted: it is certainly a genuine possibility that capitalism may yet collapse in the catastrophic manner of the late 1920s, and that all the devices improvised for enabling it to survive, from Keynesian economics to welfare reform, will prove to have been ineffectual. But we should remember that Trotsky was not speaking about an 'eventual' collapse of capitalism: anyone can say that, and almost everyone has. He was venturing more precise predictions about the historical outcome of the Second World War and, as a serious man, was prepared to risk major revisions of his thought in case he were wrong. What is more, a prediction sufficiently mistaken as to tempo becomes a prediction mistaken as to content – all societies may collapse, just as all men must die, but historical predictions have significance only insofar as they provide, approximately, time coefficients. And finally, if Western capitalism does collapse – something very different, by the way, from the recurrent troubles it goes through, for all societies go through troubles – it is far from clear or even plausible that there will follow a historical denouement of the kind that would confirm Marxist expectations or satisfy humane standards.

Nor have Trotsky's prognoses concerning Russia been realized. The post-Stalin society has achieved a relative stability: it is neither threatened by bourgeois restoration nor is it within measurable distance of socialist democracy, but maintains itself as an authoritarian dictatorship, keeping terror in reserve while not employing it with the maniacal consistency of Stalin. Trotsky would surely have hailed the appearance of the various intellectual oppositions, or democratic movements, in the Soviet Union. (It might have been deeply interesting to read him on the intellectual development of Solzhenitsyn.) But could he really have seen these heroic but isolated outbursts of moral revolt as harbingers of a 'second proletarian revolution'? Would he not have had to grapple with the problem of whether mass rebellion is possible, or in which ways it is possible, against a stable totalitarian order? Here again his Marxism would have had to show remarkable flexibility, perhaps to the point of self-transformation, in order to cope with such problems.

No political thinker can reasonably be expected to foresee every twist and turn of history; none has. The point of the criticisms suggested here is by no means to add up instances of error or to indulge in the foolishness of being what the Germans call a *besserwisser*. The point is, rather, to call into question the rightness of a comprehensive historical and political approach. And the evidence seems strongly to indicate that the whole outlook of revolutionary Marxism-Leninism as Trotsky understood it simply broke down before the realities of mid-twentieth-century political life.

Nor are Trotsky's real or apparent failures in historical prediction nearly so disturbing as his refusal, perhaps inability, to reconsider certain of his intellectual premises. In his last book, the biography of Stalin, there are perhaps one or two signs that he had begun to feel some uneasiness about the Bolshevik heritage; but for the most part he continued to defend it energetically. His powers of mind operated within a fixed political tradition, but not towards scrutinizing his own assumptions. One could hardly have expected him to repudiate his lifework, and much of the anti-Bolshevism directed against him must be acknowledged to have been crude in method and purpose. Yet for a Marxist theoretician who so fiercely and effectively criticized every move of the Stalinist regime and who so contemptuously swept aside all of its pretexts for the suppression of freedom, there should have been a stronger impetus to turn back to the early years of Bolshevism and submit them to the objective critical study that historical distance makes possible.

It is very hard to imagine that Trotsky's influence in the future will be of the kind he anticipated: a renewal of orthodox Marxism in theory and proletarian revolution in practice, along the lines known as 'Trotskyism'. The sects that continue to struggle or stagnate in his name have not been distinguished for an ability to engage in fresh thought politically or reach the masses of workers practically. We are living in times that disintegrate all fixed ideologies, and the idea of socialism, if it is to survive as more than a historical memory or a label incongruously attached to authoritarian states, will surely go through a good many transmutations and critical revisions in the coming years. Of the efforts made in Europe and America during the recent decades to bring new life to the idea of socialism – efforts ranging from the deeply impressive to the merely feckless – few if any have proceeded along the lines of orthodox Bolshevism. History brings surprises, many of them unpleasant; one may doubt that it allows repetitions of the kind Trotsky sought. And in truth, is there really any reason, even among those of us who hold firm to the socialist vision, to want a return to the orthodoxies of 'the dictatorship of the proletariat', 'the vanguard party', and other such notions? Whatever may be the fate of socialism, there does not seem to be any serious possibility in the industrialized countries of a mass movement along the lines Trotsky proposed. As for the grotesque parodies of Marxism in the 'third world', one may be reasonably certain that Trotsky would have been among the first to repudiate them. Despite Trotsky's grandiose predictions about the future of his Fourth International, Trotskyism as a political movement has for many years been without political or intellectual significance: a petrified ideology.

Nevertheless, I believe that a good portion of the writings of this extraordinary man is likely to survive and the example of his energy and heroism likely to grip the imagination of generations to come. In the East European countries heretics turn instinctively to his forbidden books, not so much for precise guidance as for a renewal of the possibility for serious debate. In the West political thinkers must confront his formidable presence, parrying his sharp polemics and learning from his significant mistakes. His greatest books transcend political dispute: they are part of the heritage of our century. For Trotsky embodied the modern historical crisis with an intensity of consciousness and a gift for heroic response which few of his contemporaries could match: he tried, on his own terms, to be equal to his time. Even those of us who cannot heed his word may recognize that Leon Trotsky, in his power and his fall, is one of the titans of our century.

Appendix

I find it impossible to write about Trotsky without adding a few words about his biographer, Isaac Deutscher. Simply as biography, Deutscher's three volumes are masterful. There is little possibility that in the near future anyone will write a life of Trotsky so authoritative, vivid, scholarly and dispassionately sympathetic. Yet throughout his work Deutscher advances a theory of Stalinism that requires serious confrontation – I would say, refutation – especially because he tends to assimilate it to Trotsky's thought. At the least, readers of Deutscher's great work ought to know at which points his ideas diverge from, indeed vulgarize, Trotsky's ideas.

In analysing the Stalinist system, Deutscher refuses to see it as a fundamental break from the socialist premises originally advanced by Lenin and Trotsky. While utterly hostile to the Stalinist terror, its forced collectivization and rape of culture, he persists in regarding the Communist state as in some sense 'progressive'. In his second volume he writes that the decades of Stalinism should be called a time of 'primitive socialist accumulation' – the latter phrase borrowed from the Trotskyist lexicon to describe a period in which a workers' state accumulates the capital needed for its growth into a classless, socialist society.

Deutscher believes that the Stalin dictatorship preserved and extended the 'conquest' of the October revolution; and on behalf of this theory he is generous with historical analogies to the French and English revolutions, by means of which Stalin is compared to revolutionary despots of the past who in corrupted form preserved the achievements of their idealistic predecessors. In the outlook that Deutscher shares with other and less gifted 'authoritarians of the left', the Stalinist regime thus becomes a tragic yet transient, a regrettable but perhaps unavoidable, episode in the building of 'socialism'.

The force of Deutscher's argument is to legitimatize Stalin as a despot who performed the cruel necessities of history. That the 'primitive socialist accumulation' of the Stalin years might in point of fact be described as a 'primitive anti-socialist accumulation' Deutscher cannot accept. That Stalin's industrialization led to a new form of authoritarian collectivism, a repressive class society neither capitalist nor socialist, Deutscher does not countenance as even a theoretical possibility.

This political outlook, with all sorts of hesitations and discomforts, remains committed to an 'essential' value of the Communist world. Usually this value is found in nationalized property, which is seen as the ultimate guarantor of progress. Where Marx spoke of 'the categorical imperative that all conditions must be revolutionized in which man is a debased, an abandoned, a contemptible being', the left authoritarians prefer to speak of the tempo of Russian industrialization or the necessary unfolding of the 'Iron Laws of History'. Where socialists have declared the possibility of a humane society to rest upon the capacity of men to act autonomously and freely, the left authoritarians put their faith in economic development as such, or in historical abstractions acting beyond, often against, the desires of living men.

Those who accept this outlook expect an orderly development, a gradual slide towards 'democratization', within the Communist world. It follows that they should have seen the 1956 East European uprising as in fact Deutscher did: 'The people of Hungary in a heroic frenzy tried unwittingly to put the clock back, while Moscow sought once again to wind up with the bayonet, or rather the tank, the broken clock of the Hungarian Communist revolution.' Here, as in his writings about Stalinism, Deutscher insists that the rebels 'unwittingly' are retrograde, perhaps counter-revolutionary, while the Communist dictatorship, however brutal, is an agency of the future. No wonder Deutscher felt small need to identify with those who in Budapest and elsewhere fought against the Russian tanks.

The whole issue is of great moral and political significance, and here Trotsky, whatever weaknesses there may be in his theory of Stalinism, is radically at odds with Deutscher. At one point, in discussing Trotsky's 1939 essay speculating on the future of humanity in case socialism should fail, Deutscher quotes Trotsky as saying, 'It is self-evident that a new minimum programme would be required – to defend the interests of the slaves of the totalitarian bureaucratic system.' Deutscher then comments:

> The passage was characteristic of the man: if bureaucratic slavery was all that the future had in store for mankind, then he . . . would be on the side of the slaves and not of the new exploiters, however 'historically necessary' the new exploitation might be. Having lived all his life with the conviction that . . . history was on the side of those who struggled for the emancipation of the exploited and oppressed, he now entreated his disciples to remain on the side of the exploited . . . even if history and all scientific certainties were against them. He, at any rate, would be with Spartacus, not with Pompey and the Caesars.

A remarkable passage! And not merely for its tribute to Trotsky's identification with the oppressed, even if they be forever doomed to oppression, but still more for the clear implication that Deutscher, who consistently upheld the 'historical necessity' of regimes like those of Stalin, might not accompany Trotsky on the tortured path of Spartacus. Given his views, there is little reason why Deutscher should.

Deutscher's theory seizes upon the authoritarian side of Trotsky's thought while de-emphasizing the revolutionary-democratic side; it yields to the abstraction of historical development or technological progress those tasks which can be won only through conscious human struggle. Deutscher suffered from a modern disease: the infatuation with history. He never learned that unpredictable as human history may be, History is a bitch.

Notes

1. Early Years, Basic Theories

1. Isaac Deutscher makes this point in somewhat different language:

> It did not occur to Trotsky that a proletarian party would in the long run rule and govern an enormous country against the majority of the people. He did not foresee that the revolution would lead to the prolonged rule of a minority. The possibility of such a rule was implicit in his theory; but its actuality would have appeared to him, as to nearly all his contemporaries, incompatible with socialism. In fact, he did not imagine, in spite of all he had written about Lenin's 'Jacobinism', that the revolution would seek to escape from its isolation and weakness into totalitarianism.

2. This point is developed by Richard Lowenthal:

> The Bolshevik party in Lenin's time, though in fact independent of working-class interests thanks to its centralist organization, was at least based on a predominantly proletarian membership and allied with important sections of the West European proletariat, whereas in the case of Mao's party today the claim to represent the industrial proletariat has become wholly fictitious: it rests neither on its history, its composition nor its international influence, only on the vestigial notion that whoever conducts a militant revolutionary struggle against imperialist monopoly capitalism expresses *ipso facto* the true class consciousness of the proletariat.
>
> Yet just in its conflict with both Marxism and Leninism, Mao's new doctrine is based on some of the decisive historical facts of our time. In the forty years since Lenin died, the workers of the advanced industrial countries have become less and less revolutionary, with the result that in no such country have the Communists been able to

lead a victorious revolutionary movement. By contrast, it is in the underdeveloped countries that huge masses of people, living in extreme insecurity on the edge of starvation, can be said to have 'nothing to lose but their chains', and their despair has offered opportunities for a number of victorious revolutions, including Communist revolutions. The course of contemporary history has thus made it impossible for the Communist leaders to be faithful to Lenin's Marxist belief in the industrial working class and to Lenin's passion for revolution struggle at the same time, though they have tried hard not to admit the fact to themselves. Under the pressure of their conflict with the Soviets, the Chinese leaders, whose links to European Marxism and to the industrial proletariat have always been tenuous, have at last made a choice: [to be] wholly revolutionary, but only marginally proletarian.

2. The Seizure of Power

1. Shortly after the 1905 revolution, in which Soviets first made their appearance, Trotsky offered a cogent description of their historical role:

The soviet of workers deputies emerged in fulfilment of an objective need – generated by the course of events – for an organization that would represent authority without containing tradition; for an organization ready to encompass the scattered masses numbering hundreds of thousands without imposing on them many organizational restraints; for an organization that would unite revolutionary currents within the proletariat, that could take the initiative and automatically control itself; and, most importantly, for an organization that could be created within 24 hours.

Trotsky wrote these lines before he became a Bolshevik: they contained nothing about the 'hegemony' or 'guidance' of the vanguard party.

2. This point is largely supported by the veteran Menshevik leader Raphael Abramovitch in his book *The Soviet Revolu-*

tion. The Provisional Government, he writes, 'could not do the one thing that might have preserved the esteem of the masses – namely, launch an energetic and unequivocal drive for peace. The leadership of the Menshevik defencists and of the SRs still wished to maintain the coalition with the liberal bourgeois groups and maintain harmony in the Allied camp.'

3. Trotsky returned to this theme several times, trying to find ways of reconciling his Marxism with his perception of Lenin's decisive role. In his diary for March 1935 he writes:

> Had I not been present in 1917 in Petersburg, the October Revolution would still have taken place – *on the condition that Lenin was present and in command.* If neither Lenin nor I had been present in Petersburg, there would have been no October Revolution : the leadership of the Bolshevik Party would have prevented it from occurring – of this I have not the slightest doubt! ∕

What then happens to historical materialism, to say nothing of the elaborate analysis offered by Trotsky in his various works intended to show the Bolshevik revolution as a necessary outcome of Russian development?

4. Sukhanov, the Menshevik memoirist, writes that in leaving the Congress the Mensheviks and SRs 'completely untied the Bolsheviks' hands, making them masters of the entire situation and yielding to them the entire arena of the revolution. A struggle at the Congress for a united democratic front *might* have had some success . . . By quitting the Congress, we ourselves gave the Bolsheviks a monopoly of the Soviet, of the masses, and of the revolution.'

3. Bolshevism Overreaches Itself

1. In the late 1930s Trotsky once remarked scornfully at the argument of the French writer Henri Barbusse that

Stalin's victory over Trotsky showed that Stalin had been right. This, scoffed Trotsky, was a good way of justifying . . . Hitler. In scoring this point against the not-very-brilliant Barbusse, did Trotsky perhaps remember what he had written in *Terrorism and Communism*?

2. Trotsky coined a graphic phrase for describing the peasants' reaction: they were for 'the Bolsheviks' who had driven off the landowners, they were against 'the Communists' who forcibly requisitioned their surpluses — and sometimes more than surpluses.

4. The Rise of Stalinism

1. Which, in a fuller account of Trotsky's career, would have to be discussed in detail. Trotsky wrote and spoke voluminously on events in Germany and France during these years, urging a flexible application of Bolshevik strategy but never questioning whether that strategy was at all applicable to Western countries. Try as they might, the Russian Bolsheviks found it hard not to adopt a somewhat tutorial relation towards their European disciples — some of whom were not, in any case, very bright pupils. It was characteristic of Trotsky's thought at this time, indeed of Bolshevik thought in general, that it should display ingenuity in the elaboration of secondary analysis but harden increasingly in its assertion of primary assumptions.

2. Given the poverty of the time, a 'rich' peasant often meant one who owned a horse and could afford to hire an occasional or part-time labourer.

3. It may help some readers if I provide in this note the barest outline of the history of intra-Bolshevik factional struggles during the 1920s, while leaving the political and ideological issues for the text itself.

Even before Lenin died there had formed at the top of the party a faction or clique led by veteran functionaries who had worked for many years in the party apparatus. At its head stood 'the Troika', Stalin, Zinoviev, Kamenev, anxious to keep Trotsky from assuming party leadership if Lenin died. Bitter intrigues followed in which Trotsky was steadily defeated, partly because he was still seen as a newcomer or interloper in the Bolshevik hierarchy, partly because he underestimated the capacities of the bureaucratic formation that Stalin led, and partly because the increasingly weary and demoralized atmosphere of the country (also of the party) favoured the conservative drift of the Troika.

In the autumn of 1923 a group of 46 prominent Bolsheviks, including such leaders as Pyatakov, Preobrazhensky, Muralov, Ivan Smirnov and Antonov-Ovseenko, issued a full-scale statement attacking the Troika, calling for balanced economic planning, and demanding a reinvigoration of party democracy. This marks, more or less, the moment at which the Left Opposition, or the Trotskyists, came formally into being. The Left Opposition was never a close-knit faction, but it numbered in its ranks many of the most intellectually accomplished and respected figures of Bolshevism. Among the youth it also won considerable support.

Alarmed, the Stalin-Zinoviev-Kamenev group now began a sustained and increasingly brutal assault not only on the Trotskyists but upon all expressions of dissident opinion within the party. At every point, the machine beat down the Left Opposition, depriving its leaders of their posts and threatening rank-and-file sympathizers with punitive measures. The battle of articles, speeches and polemics continued until about 1926 when Trotsky acknowledged his defeat and assumed a posture of quiet waiting. In effect, the Left Opposition was disbanded, though its leaders continued to maintain intellectual contact. They feared that if they pressed their struggle any further, they would be expelled from the party and thereby debarred from political life.

Meanwhile, a split was taking place within the Troika. Frightened by the power that Stalin was gathering into his hands and fearing that with the decisive defeat of Trotsky

Stalin would no longer need them, Zinoviev and Kamenev began to rally their still considerable following. In April 1926 Trotsky, Zinoviev and Kamenev met privately, for the first time in several years, and the two former allies of Stalin expressed their fears of Stalin's cruelty and power-lust. They seem then to have grasped the character of the future dictator better than Trotsky did. In any case, a new bloc, the Joint Opposition, was soon formed, bringing together most of the dissidents within the party. It is estimated that perhaps 8000 party members subscribed to the Joint Opposition, but since it had now become hazardous to disagree with the official leadership, it is probable that the number of sympathizers was considerably larger. The nominal membership of the party was now 750,000, but most of these were new, politically unsophisticated, and accustomed to the passive obedience which had become the party norm. Deutscher estimates that not more than 20,000 people were actively engaged in the inner-party struggles.

The Joint Opposition fared no better than the earlier Left Opposition. By now the party machine was largely in Stalin's hands; openly authoritarian and repressive practices had become commonplace; both the morals and morale of the Bolshevik cadres had sunk to a low point. When Opposition leaders tried to speak to factory workers, they were forcibly prevented.

Within months, the organizational spine of the Joint Opposition was broken by Stalin's machine and a formal capitulation, though not a rescinding of opinion, followed. Nevertheless, the struggle continued for a time, until at the end of 1927 1500 Trotskyists were expelled from the party. Most of the Zinovievists surrendered. In early 1928 Trotsky was sent into exile, as were many other party dissidents.

There would be one other open political battle, that between Stalin and his ally of yesterday, Bukharin, now leader of a group of Right Communists. By mid-1929 this dispute came to an end with the victory of Stalin and the break-up of the Bukharin group.

A few clandestine intra-party efforts were made in the

1930s to organize opposition to the Stalin dictatorship; all failed.

4. One of the more depressing incidents concerns 'Lenin's testament', in which the Bolshevik leader had appraised the major figures surrounding him and then proposed that Stalin be removed as General Secretary. This document had been suppressed after Lenin's death; but in 1925 the American radical writer Max Eastman, in his book *Since Lenin Died*, gave an accurate version of what Lenin had written. When the Politbureau of the Bolshevik party, dominated by Stalin, insisted that Trotsky issue a public denial of what Eastman had written, 'the leading group of the Opposition', Trotsky later explained, felt that since it did not wish to enter battle on this matter, Trotsky should acquiesce. Trotsky thereupon signed the humiliating statement that 'all talk about [Lenin's] "testament", allegedly suppressed or violated, is a malicious invention . . .' This was neither the first nor last 'necessary lie' told by political leaders of all varieties; but for Trotsky it was especially galling. For many years, by the way, the official Communist press throughout the world kept reprinting Trotsky's 1925 statement, even though it was common knowledge that he had signed it under duress.

5. A biographer of Trotsky, unsympathetic but in this instance shrewd, remarks:

> It was no doubt his lofty – indeed, in the philosophical sense 'idealist' view of politics that made Trotsky misunderstand what was actually happening . . . It astigmatized him, as it were, with respect to the power of the actual apparatus, and made him regard himself as a Bolshevik paragon merely because of his identification with the Idea of the Party : he disregarded his failure to be identified with its *personnel*. [Joel Carmichael, *Trotsky*.]

6. In these articles Trotsky was both recapitulating traditional Marxist views on bureaucratism and sometimes grappling, it seems, towards a theory that would explain

it as more than a derivation from social scarcity and class rule. I quote a few lines:

> It is unworthy of a Marxist to consider that bureaucratism is only the aggregate of the bad habits of office holders. Bureaucratism is a social phenomenon in that it is a definite system of administration of men and things. Its profound causes lie in the heterogeneity of society, the difference between the daily and the fundamental interests of various groups of the population. Bureaucratism is complicated by the fact of the lack of culture of the broad masses. With us, the essential source of bureaucratism resides in the necessity of creating and sustaining a state apparatus that unites the interests of the proletariat and those of the peasantry in a perfect economic harmony, from which we are still far removed. The necessity of maintaining a permanent army is likewise another important source of bureaucratism.

7. A good many of Trotsky's colleagues, chafing in exile, were sufficiently impressed with this industrialization to recant their opposition and offer obeisance to the Stalin regime. Many of them, like Preobrazhensky himself, came back from exile and took posts of varying, but never primary, importance in the regime. By the end of the 1930s, they had all paid for this decision with their heads.

8. This point is discussed at persuasive length in Stephen F. Cohen's *Bukharin and the Bolshevik Revolution*, a study that must be consulted by anyone interested in the outcome of Bolshevism.

5. Wandering, Exile, Work

1. I diverge from my subject to recount an incident that seems worth keeping in memory. A friend of mine and life-long socialist, Lewis Coser, attended some years ago an academic reception in Cambridge, Massachusetts. To his astonishment he was introduced to a man named Mark

Zborowski, by then exposed as a GPU agent known to have played a part in the death of Rudolph Klement, a young Trotskyist in Paris. In an act of disciplined revulsion, Coser refused to shake Zborowski's hand – and for this earned the disapproval of a number of liberal academics who were present. That Zborowski was a man whose past was shameful, perhaps spotted with blood, did not disturb them as much, apparently, as did Coser's 'ungentlemanly' behaviour. It took a long time for some liberals to learn the truth about Stalinism; some never have.

2. This policy followed from one of Stalin's observations: 'Fascism is the militant organization of the bourgeoisie which bases itself on the active support of Social Democracy. Objectively, Social Democracy is the moderate wing of fascism . . . These organizations do not contradict but supplement one another. They are not antipodes but twins.' There could hardly be a more telling instance of how, in Voltaire's words, absurdity leads to atrocity.

6. Final Legacy

1. This record yields some interesting evidence on Trotsky's later thought. In response to a question from Finerty as to whether a revolutionary government had a right to resort to terror, Trotsky replied: 'It is not an abstract right. I hope that after one or two victories in other countries the revolutions will become absolutely friendly revolutions.' Finerty: 'Bloodless revolutions?' Trotsky: 'Bloodless revolutions; yes. But the pioneers were everywhere severe people. I believe that the Americans know that better than myself.'

2. In the course of his research Professor Nedava interviewed Mrs Beba Idelson, a Jewish socialist-Zionist leader in Palestine, who visited Trotsky in Mexico. In her recollections Mrs Idelson reports that 'I talked to him not as one talks to a stranger. A feeling accompanied me all the time that he was a Jew, a wandering Jew, without a

fatherland.' For three hours Trotsky asked her sharp questions about the politics and economics of Jewish settlement. When Mrs Idelson asked him, 'Here is a country that is ready to admit you; perhaps you, too, will go to Palestine,' he replied calmly, 'Wouldn't you be afraid to accept me?' To which she answered: 'No, we won't be afraid, for our idea is stronger than any fear of any man, even of a man like you.' Trotsky was evidently touched by her sincerity and at the end of their talk asked Mrs Idelson to 'let the matter remain between us. The world will not understand.' She waited nineteen years before telling her story.

What 'the world will not understand' no one can be quite certain. Still, it is a thought to conjure with that if Trotsky had lived some years longer he too would have been eligible to come to the new state of Israel under 'the Law of Return'.

3. Other writers on the left, like the distinguished economist of the Austrian Social Democracy Rudolf Hilferding, and later the Yugoslav ex-Communist Milovan Djilas, and the little-known American socialist Joseph Carter, developed similar theories.

Short Bibliography

Trotsky's Works

Trotsky's writings are now being systematically reprinted by publishing houses sympathetic to his ideas: Pathfinder Press in New York City (410 West Street, NYC 10014) and Pathfinder Press in London (47 The Cut, London, SE1 8LL). These houses have issued reprints not only of most of Trotsky's major works, especially those that had gone out of print or not been available, but also have brought together large portions of his previously untranslated and/or uncollected writings in special volumes arranged according to topic or time.

Listed below are some of the major works by Trotsky that are now in print. Unless otherwise indicated, these are available in Pathfinder editions. The dates are those of the most recent printing:

Our Revolution. Henry Holt, 1918.

1905. Random House, 1972.

Terrorism and Communism. University of Michigan Press, 1972.

Lessons of October. New Park Publications (London), 1971.

The New Course. University of Michigan Press, 1965.

Literature and Revolution. Russell & Russell, 1957.

The First Five Years of the Communist International (2 vols.)

The Permanent Revolution

The Third International After Lenin

The Real Situation in Russia. Harcourt, Brace, 1928.

The History of the Russian Revolution (3 vols.). University of Michigan Press, 1960.

My Life

The Revolution Betrayed

Stalin. Harper & Bros., 1946.

Their Morals and Ours

Whither France?
Diary in Exile. Harvard University Press, 1958.

A number of useful collections and anthologies of Trotsky's writings are also available:
Writings of Leon Trotsky (12 vols.)
On Literature and Art
On the Jewish Question

The Basic Writings of Trotsky, ed. Irving Howe. Random House, 1963.
The Age of Permanent Revolution, ed. Isaac Deutscher. Dell, 1964.

Books about Trotsky

Biography
Eastman, Max, *Leon Trotsky: The Portrait of a Youth.* Greenberg, 1925.
Deutscher, Isaac, *The Prophet Armed.* Oxford University Press, 1954.
Deutscher, Isaac, *The Prophet Unarmed.* Oxford University Press, 1959.
Deutscher, Isaac, *The Prophet Outcast.* Oxford University Press, 1963.
Serge, Victor, and Trotsky, Natalya Sedova, *The Life and Death of Leon Trotsky.* Basic Books, 1975; Wildwood House, 1975.

Discussion and Criticism of Ideas
The literature on the Russian Revolution, Bolshevism, Trotsky, Stalinism, etc., is vast, but only a small part of it warrants the attention of the serious reader. Below is a short list of books, written from many different points of view, that do merit attention:
Abramovitch, Raphael, *The Soviet Revolution, 1961.* International Universities Press, 1960.
Cohen, Stephen, *Bukharin and the Bolshevik Revolution.* Knopf, 1973; Wildwood House, 1974.

Day, Robert, *Leon Trotsky and the Politics of Economic Isolation.* Cambridge University Press, 1973.

Erlich, Alexander, *The Soviet Industrialization Debate, 1924–1928.* Harvard University Press, 1960.

Medvedev, Roy, *Let History Judge.* Knopf, 1972; Macmillan, 1972.

Nedava, Joseph, *Trotsky and the Jews.* Jewish Publication Society of America, 1970.

Schapiro, Leonard, *The Origins of the Communist Autocracy.* Harvard University Press, 1955.

Shachtman, Max, *The Bureaucratic Revolution.* Donald Press, 1962.

Souvarine, Boris, *Stalin.* Longman, Green, 1939.

Sukhanov, N. N., *The Russian Revolution, 1917.* Oxford University Press, 1955.

Tucker, Robert C., ed., *Stalinism: Essays in Interpretation.* Norton, 1977.

Wilson, Edmund, *To the Finland Station.* Doubleday, 1953; Fontana, 1960.

Wolfe, Bertram D., *Three Who Made a Revolution.* Dial, 1948.